LASAGNE

Also by Clifford A. Wright

Cucina Rapida
Cucina Paradiso

LASAGNE

Clifford A. Wright

Little, Brown and Company

Boston   New York   Toronto   London

First Edition

Library of Congress Cataloging-in-Publication Data
Wright, Clifford A.
    Lasagne / Clifford A. Wright.— 1st ed.
        p.   cm.
    Includes index.
    ISBN 0-316-95640-6
    1. Cookery (Pasta)   2. Cookery, Italian.   I. Title
TX809.M17W75   1995   94-3495
641.8' 22—dc20

10 9 8 7 6 5 4 3 2 1

R R D - V A

Designed by Barbara Werden

Published simultaneously in Canada by
Little, Brown & Company (Canada) Limited

Printed in the United States of America

Dedicated to the little lasagne eaters:

Ali Kattan-Wright
Dyala Kattan-Wright
Seri Kattan-Wright
Rachel Irwin
Nathan Irwin
Emma Sherwood-Forbes
Duncan Sherwood-Forbes
Alex Stange
Mia Stange

CONTENTS

ACKNOWLEDGMENTS

I PERSONALLY test all my recipes, because I love to cook and to assure my readers of a cookbook that works. Writing a book about lasagne meant testing and eating a lot of lasagne. There was more lasagne than my children and I could eat, and I was lucky to have some great friends who with their children shared many lasagne, helped buy food, and never once complained about eating so much lasagne. There were times when we would sit down after a marathon recipe-testing day and have first, second, and third courses, all lasagne. We ate lasagne until it came out of our ears, and incredibly, we never tired of it. In fact, we were amazed that the lasagne were so consistently good. This isn't bragging—it's a testament to how universally good lasagne are, how easy they are to make and serve, and how they are the quintessential family comfort food.

This book would not have been nearly as much fun to write without my very good friends David Forbes, Virginia Sherwood, Eric Stange, Barbara Costa, Harry Irwin, and Pam Haltom, and their children, to whom the book is dedicated.

Without the memories of the lasagne made by my mom, Helen DeYeso Wright, and the joy of having my dad, Harold Wright, as my dad, who took us all over Europe and made us laugh, this book would never be.

I also want to thank my agent, Doe Coover, for working her magic; my editor, Jennifer Josephy, for her insight and enthusiasm; and my copyeditor, Deborah Jacobs, for the most extraordinary job of copyediting I've ever seen, period.

LASAGNE

INTRODUCTION

THE IDEA for a lasagne cookbook came to me several years ago while I was in Italy researching another book. All over Italy I stumbled across lasagne recipes. Each one was different and delicious. For years the only lasagne I had known was my mother's meat sauce, ricotta, and mozzarella dish. But during my travels in Italy I discovered a wealth of regional favorites such as the light and flavorful spinach lasagne of Emilia-Romagna, Lasagne Verdi al Forno (page 53), leaf-thin sheets of green lasagne delicately moistened with a mere film of béchamel sauce. In the Veneto region I came across Lasagne al Fornel (page 66), with its unusual mixture of apples, golden raisins, walnuts, and dried figs, served as a first course and not a dessert. In Sicily I encountered the heavenly Lasagne alla Catanese (page 59), studded with eggplant, olives, yellow sweet peppers, and capers.

I also found a world of lasagne dishes that were not baked — simply tossed or layered with sauces, such as the delectable Lasagne di San Giuseppe (page 93), feathery, translucent sheets of lasagne with fried bread crumbs, ground almonds, anchovies, tomatoes, and fresh basil.

When I was growing up, one of the few dishes my mother would make that demonstrated her Italian heritage was her lasagna, called and spelled *lasagna*. (*Lasagna* is singular and *lasagne* is plural in Italian.) In those days —

the fifties and sixties—we knew nothing about fresh lasagne, fresh ricotta, fresh mozzarella, and for that matter fresh anything. But it was great.

This standard recipe that we all know, with its ragù, ricotta, and mozzarella, also happens to be the limit of most American cooks' experience with lasagne. It is merely Neapolitan-style lasagne, and a very good one at that.

In Italy, however, lasagne is not a single recipe but many preparations, all using sheets of dough made either with durum wheat and water or with white flour and eggs, and layered (or not) with a wide variety of fillings, sauces, and cheeses.

In Italian the word *lasagne* also means the sheets of pasta. As best I can make out, any pasta sheet longer than 2 inches and wider than 1 inch is what an Italian means by lasagne. Between ¾ inch and 1 inch it seems to be called lasagnette. *Lasagne ricce* or *doppio ricce* are sheets of lasagne with one or two ruffled edges.

THE HISTORY OF LASAGNE

The origin of lasagne, macaroni, spaghetti, and the rest—what the Italians call *pasta secca* (dried hard-wheat pasta) or simply *macche-rone*—is wrapped in myth. We thought until recently that Marco Polo introduced macaroni to Italy upon his return from China in 1295. In his travel diaries from Sumatra he described a dough made of breadfruit flour that he called *lagana,* a Latin word that meant a kind of thin crêpe in the thirteenth century and is still used today in Calabria for a wide tagliatelle. And in Greece it is the name of a Lenten bread that was once unleavened.

Some people say the Romans invented macaroni, arguing that the Latin lagana is none other than *lasagne.* But the works of Horace, Celsus, Apicius, and Petronius, where the word *lagana* appears in such various forms as *laganum* and *lasanum,* show that it doesn't mean pasta secca as we know it. Lasanum, derived from the Greek *lasanon,* a chamber pot or cooking pot, seems to refer to a kind of cake or crêpe made of flour and oil that is deep-fried.

Pasta secca was unknown in Roman times because hard wheat was probably unknown or little known. The Romans used soft wheat, known as emmer or poulard. In any case, this isn't the final word—the question of whether durum wheat was known in classical times is hotly debated by scholars. The debate will continue because paleobotany is not an exact science, and every possible viewpoint has found an advocate.

I don't believe mixing flour and water is unique. What is unique about pasta secca is that it is made out of a certain kind of wheat, called hard wheat or durum wheat, which has the singular property of a high-gluten and low-moisture content. This property led to the invention of food products that were important not because of their shape, or because of the method of processing, but because they were durable. Durability of food was important in the Middle Ages because of the frequent threat of famine. Hard-wheat food products could be warehoused to counteract years of low production and to offset inflation caused by high prices and demand. In addition, the invention of durable hard-wheat products such as pasta secca, couscous, and hardtack allowed longer sea voyages, opening up an age of exploration.

In the ninth or tenth century the Arabs brought durum wheat to Sicily, where it replaced the soft wheat of the Romans. Gradually, hard wheat dispersed to the Italian peninsula over the next few hundred years. One of the very first pasta products ever made with hard wheat was lasagne.

An intriguing new line on the history of lasagne has been proposed by several French scholars. They suggest that *lasagne* may be derived from the medieval Arabic word *lawzinaj* or *losange,* from which we get *lozenge. Losange* meant a thin cake of pastry, usually made with almonds. This cake was cut into ribbons, quadrangles, and rhomboids. A fifteenth-century cookery manuscript, known as "Libro B di Anonimo Meridionale" and held in a private collection in Stockholm, used for one recipe the title *alesagne,* which appears to retain the Arabic definite article *al.*

By the early fourteenth century, pasta in all its forms was known in Italy. The oldest written use in Italian of *macaroni* to mean pasta secca is in a notary document from Genoa dated 1279, which listed a chest of macaroni among the possessions of a soldier named Ponzio Bastone. But more than a century before this document was written and before Marco Polo's return from China, macaroni is known to have existed in Sicily. Al-Edrisi, the Arab court geographer of the Norman king Roger II in Palermo, wrote in 1154 in his book *Kitab ar-Ruger* of huge quantities of *itriya*—vermicelli, a form of pasta secca—being made in Sicily. This medieval Arabic word survives in Sicily today as *tria,* a kind of spaghetti.

The first written references to what might be pasta secca are in the ninth-century dictionary of Isho Bar Ali, a Syrian lexicographer, who described itriya as a pasta made from semolina that resembled a cloth—which sounds very much like lasagne. We can't be sure that he meant a semolina of hard wheat, but it looks promising.

Lasagne begins to be mentioned by name for the first time, and not elliptically, in the fourteenth century. A document in the archives of Palermo from 1371 stated that macaroni and lasagne were triple the price of bread. Earlier still, one of the first descriptions of pasta in the form of lasagne is in the anonymous thirteenth-century Hispano-Muslim cookery book *Kitab al-Tabikh fi al-Maghrib wal-Andalus,* which has several entries about *al-fidawash,* a variety of pasta. It was said to be made in several forms: long strips, tiny spheres, and thin paperlike sheets.

In Italy one of the very first words to describe pasta secca was *maccherone* (macaroni), a word commonly thought to have originated in the Naples area in the eleventh century. Today macaroni usually refers to a tubular pasta about 1¾ inches long. Where does this word come from? I believe that the etymology, usually thought to be Greek or obscure, may be Arabic. A very old pasta form known in Tunisia is *dwida,* meaning inchworm, a vermicelli broken into one-inch lengths. When you take the two ends of the strand of *dwida* and attach them, they are called *qaran,* from the Arabic verb *qarana,* to attach. Something that is attached would take the prefix *ma,* and this kind of pasta is called *maqrun* or *maqaruna,* the adjective form.

The first written Italian lasagne recipe is found in an anonymous fourteenth-century cookery manuscript from the Angevin court in Naples called *Liber de Coquina.* The sheets of lasagne are boiled and layered with ground spices and grated cheese in a bowl or trencher. In such medieval recipes, spices can mean salt and pepper or sugar, or some combination such as salt, pepper, cinnamon, cloves, nutmeg, and maybe saffron.

The following recipe is my version of another early lasagne recipe, from the *Libro della Cocina,* also an anonymous work, by a Tuscan of the fourteenth century.

 # DE LA LASANIS

1 recipe Homemade Durum-Wheat and Water Lasagne (page 12)
1 recipe Chicken Broth (page 28)
1 cup freshly grated Parmigiano-Reggiano cheese
Freshly ground black pepper

1. Prepare the lasagne.
2. Prepare the chicken broth.
3. Bring the broth to a rolling boil. Salt if necessary and drop the lasagne in gradually. Drain the lasagne when al dente and transfer to individual bowls, sheet by sheet, with a sprinkling of Parmigiano-Reggiano in between. Ladle some of the broth over and serve with a sprinkling of pepper.

Serves 4 to 6

1

THE BASICS

JUST AS there are two basic types of lasagne dishes, baked and simply tossed with other ingredients, there are two basic lasagne pastas you can use: commercially made, store-bought lasagne and homemade lasagne.

Commercially made lasagne is either domestically produced or imported from Italy. Both imported and domestic lasagne can also be divided into "instant" — that is, no-boil — and regular. What I call regular lasagne is simply the lasagne you are familiar with, which needs to be parboiled before baking. I find this regular lasagne much too thick, so I always use either the imported or domestic instant lasagne, distinguished by being translucent: when you hold a sheet of it up in front of your hand, you can see your fingers through it. This no-boil lasagne is a superior pasta product, not only in taste but in convenience. Ask the manager of your local supermarket to carry it. I mention some manufacturers below (see pages 15–16).

Commercial lasagne can be used in all the recipes, although I will occasionally suggest you give homemade lasagne a try. In no recipe is this essential, however — it's simply a matter of taste.

But this matter of taste can be crucial. Homemade lasagne is on a plateau of taste far above commercially made lasagne. In fact, I am tempted to be snobbish and say you should always use homemade lasagne. The only reason

I don't is that the imported, thin, no-boil lasagne is a close second.

There is nothing intrinsically hard about making your own pasta. Not only is it worth the effort, I venture that it will be the best pasta you've tasted. You may be quite unhappy about buying commercial pasta ever again, so beware.

I find making my own pasta, as with my own bread, a relaxing, therapeutic activity, and not a chore at all. Well, that's not really true — it is a chore, but a delicious one. Every time I make lasagne I agonize over taste versus time. Of course, there are many electric pasta-making machines on the market that solve this problem, although generally they do not knead the dough sufficiently to develop the gluten in durum wheat. But if you don't have one, read on.

You may be reluctant to make your own lasagne because of the time required or past failures. I know this feeling, since I once was a beginner and regularly failed at making pasta. After much experimentation I have come to the recipes in this chapter (pages 10–14), which work for me every time — and they should for you too.

FROM SCRATCH: BASIC TECHNIQUE FOR HOMEMADE LASAGNE

The following are the equipment and ingredients you will need:

- A countertop at least 30 inches wide by 24 inches deep
- A hand-cranked or electric pasta-rolling machine or a *matterello,* a rolling pin at least 24 inches long
- A standard rolling pin
- Wax paper or plastic wrap
- Paper towels, white kitchen towels, a white top sheet, or an expandable spare window screen
- A kitchen table that no one will be using for about 2 hours
- Durum-wheat flour and/or all-purpose bleached or unbleached white flour
- Eggs
- Water
- Salt
- Olive oil
- A knife for cutting the lasagne sheets
- A large baking tray for dredging the lasagne in flour

There are five basic steps in making your own lasagne: mixing, kneading, rolling, cutting, and drying.

Mixing by Hand

See step 1 for Homemade White Flour and Egg Lasagne (page 10) or Homemade Durum-Wheat and Water Lasagne (page 12).

Mixing with a Heavy-Duty Electric Mixer

Attach the flat beater to the mixer. Pour in the flour and start on low. Add 1 egg (if making White Flour and Egg Lasagne) or one third of the water (if making Durum-Wheat and Water

Lasagne) and mix for 2 minutes. Continue adding the eggs or one-third measures of water at 2-minute intervals. When the last egg or one third of the water has been incorporated, the dough will be lumpy.

Kneading

Dump the dough onto a floured work surface and finish kneading by hand until you have a ball that is elastic but firm and shiny. If the dough ball is too hard, wet your hands and knead some more. If it is too soft, dust with flour and knead some more. Wrap the ball in wax paper or plastic wrap. For White Flour and Egg Lasagne, let rest at room temperature for 30 minutes to 1 hour; for Durum-Wheat and Water Lasagne, refrigerate 1 Hour. See the instructions in the recipes on pages 11 and 12 for more guidance on kneading.

Rolling by Machine

Pasta-rolling machines, as opposed to pasta-making machines, are hand-cranked or electric rollers that roll thin the pasta previously made by hand or in an electric mixer. They are widely available, not expensive, and worth having. The rolling process continues, in a fashion, the kneading process, meaning that you need to knead less than when doing everything by hand.

Unwrap the resting pasta dough and push down with your hand. With a rolling pin, continue rolling until the dough forms a rough circle about 12 inches in diameter. Divide into thirds, covering two thirds with the wax paper or plastic wrap. Take the remaining third and roll it through the widest setting of the rollers. After reducing the setting by another notch and rolling it through, fold in thirds so that you have a nicely shaped rectangle. You need to do this only once. Reduce the setting another notch and continue rolling, ratcheting down the rollers until you have your desired thickness. As you roll, remember to flour both sides at the slightest sign of stickiness.

Rolling by Hand

You must be a complete fanatic to want to roll pasta by hand. It's a pain in the neck, and I can't see the point of struggling with a rolling pin when a pasta-rolling machine will do the job, unless of course you are following the "therapeutic" concept mentioned above. Should you wish to roll the dough by hand, you need a long (at least 24 inches) rolling pin called a *matterello,* rather than the standard rolling pin with handles. Dust the work surface with flour and flatten the ball of dough with the palm of your hand. Start rolling away from you. Rotate and roll, continuing in this manner so that the dough forms a rough circle. Continue rolling until the dough is very thin, about $\frac{1}{16}$ inch.

At this point the dough needs to be stretched (a job the pasta-rolling machine does magnificently). Place the rolling pin horizontally across the top of the circle of dough. Make sure the dough is dusted with flour. Grab the very tip of the dough and pull it over the rolling pin. Roll the pin toward you until about one third of the dough has been rolled up. Place the palms of your hands close together in the center of the rolling pin and press down hard, rolling back and forth as your hands travel to the outer edges of the rolling pin and back to the center, as when you made snakes with Play-Doh as a child. Do this three times and then unroll the dough. Now roll another third of the dough up and repeat. Unroll the dough and rotate it so that the bottom is now at the top. Repeat the rolling process. Do the entire rolling-and-rotating procedure about four times, making sure you dust continually with flour.

Cutting and Drying

In a large baking tray, sprinkle some flour. Cut the dough into your desired shape or the shape called for in the recipe, drag it in the flour to dust, and set aside at one end of the tray while you continue rolling and cutting the rest of the dough. *Remember to always dust with flour; otherwise the sheet of lasagne will become hopelessly stuck together.* Arrange the cut pieces of lasagne on paper or kitchen towels or a white sheet to dry.

For fresh pasta, let the lasagne dry for 1 hour. You can either cook the lasagne at this point, refrigerate it, freeze it, or let it dry completely over two days and then package and store for later use as pastasciutta or pasta secca, dry pasta.

Homemade Lasagne Recipes

Most failures in pasta making come about because too much liquid is used. When it appears that the dough won't hold together, many people add more water and/or eggs — too much — and the pasta becomes brittle when dried. At first, when kneading the dough with water or eggs, my recipes may seem to be lacking in liquid. But they are not. You will still have to flour the dough once you are rolling it to keep it from sticking.

 # HOMEMADE WHITE FLOUR AND EGG LASAGNE

In southern Italy, lasagne was traditionally made only with hard-wheat flour and water. Today, as in the north, more and more cooks make pasta with eggs and white flour. Some people add a tablespoon or two of olive oil while mixing the dough.

> *3 cups all-purpose bleached or unbleached white flour*
> *3 large eggs*
> *1 teaspoon salt*
> *1 tablespoon olive oil (optional)*
> *Water as needed*
> *Flour for dusting*

1. Pour the flour onto a work surface. Make a well in the middle, piling up the flour around

it so that it resembles the walls of a volcanic crater. Break the eggs into the well, sprinkle in the salt, and drizzle in the olive oil, if using. (Add any other ingredient for colored lasagne at this point; see pages 13–14.) Break the yolks with your fingers and begin to incorporate the eggs with the flour a little at a time, with your fingers, drawing more flour from the inside wall of the well. Make sure you don't break through the wall or the eggs will run. Scrape off any dough on your fingers and knead into the dough.

2. Once the flour and eggs are combined and you can form the dough into a ball, knead for about 8 to 10 minutes (see Note). As you press down while kneading, use the ball to pick up any loose clumps of dough. Don't add any liquid until you've kneaded for at least 3 minutes. If the dough is too dry at this point and you must add water, do so only by wetting your hands, as many times as you need. If the dough is too wet — meaning if there is any sign of stickiness — dust with flour. Continue kneading, pressing down with the full force of both palms, until a smooth ball is formed. Wrap the dough in wax paper or plastic wrap and leave for 30 minutes to 1 hour at room temperature.

3. Unwrap the ball of dough and dust with flour. Place on a floured surface, pressing down with your palms to flatten. With a rolling pin, roll the pasta out until it is about 12 inches in diameter and cut it into thirds. Roll each third with the rolling pin until it is thin enough to fit into the widest setting of a pasta-rolling machine. Roll once at the widest setting. Close

the setting one notch and roll again. Gather the sheet of pasta, fold in thirds, and roll through the roller so you have a nice rectangle.

Continue ratcheting down the setting until the dough reaches the thickness you prefer or that is called for in the recipe. Dust the dough on both sides with flour at the slightest sign of stickiness. If necessary, continue to dust with flour as you roll through narrower and narrower settings; otherwise the dough will become hopelessly stuck together. By this time you will have a very long thin sheet of pliable dough that looks and even feels like a velvety chamois cloth.

4. Cut the ribbon into 6- to 12-inch lengths, 2 to 5 inches wide, unless the recipe specifies another size. Sprinkle some flour in a large baking tray and dust each length of cut lasagne on both sides with the flour. Let rest in an airy place on paper towels, white kitchen towels, or a white sheet reserved for this purpose for 1 to 2 hours before cooking, refrigerating, or freezing. Leave for 48 hours for completely dry pasta.

Note: Eight to 10 minutes of kneading is sufficient if you plan to use a hand-cranked or electric pasta-rolling machine. If you are rolling by hand, knead for another 8 minutes.

◈ HOMEMADE DURUM-WHEAT AND WATER LASAGNE

Because durum-wheat dough becomes harder and drier than one made with all-purpose bleached flour, unbleached durum-wheat and water pasta is the hardest to manipulate. Many people use a heavy-duty electric mixer, although I've had good results mixing this dough by hand.

Durum wheat is sometimes sold in supermarkets under the label "pasta flour," but check the package to be sure it is durum wheat. A. Zerega and Sons sells a product called Antoine's Pasta Flour, an enriched golden semolina of durum wheat. Bulk durum wheat can also be found through wholesalers, health food stores, and Italian grocery stores and markets. This too is an enriched product and is a yellowish-white flour.

3 cups durum-wheat flour
1 teaspoon salt
2 tablespoons olive oil
1 cup warm water

1. Pour the flour onto a work surface. Make a well in the middle, piling up the flour around it so that it resembles the walls of a volcanic crater. Sprinkle the salt into the well and slowly pour in the olive oil and water. Begin to incorporate the flour a little at a time, with your fingers, drawing more flour from the inside wall of the well. Make sure you don't break through the wall or the oil and water will run. Scrape off any dough on your fingers and knead into the dough.

2. Once the flour and water are combined and you can form the dough into a ball, knead for 8 to 10 minutes (see Note). Do not add water. As you press down while kneading, use the ball to pick up any loose clumps of dough. If you must add more water, do so only by wetting your hands, as many times as you need to. Continue kneading until a smooth ball is formed. Wrap the dough in plastic wrap and refrigerate for 1 hour.

3. Unwrap the ball of dough and dust with flour if it is sticky. On a floured surface press the ball down with the palms of your hands. With a rolling pin, roll the pasta out until it is about 12 inches in diameter and cut it into thirds. Roll each third with the rolling pin until it is thin enough to fit into the widest setting of a pasta-rolling machine. Roll once at the widest setting. Close the setting one notch and roll again. Gather the sheet of pasta, fold in thirds, and roll through the roller so you have a nice rectangle.

Note: Ten minutes of kneading is sufficient if you plan to use a hand-cranked or electric pasta-rolling machine. If you are rolling by hand, knead for another 8 minutes.

Continue ratcheting down the setting until the dough reaches the thickness you prefer or that is called for in the recipe. Dust the dough with flour on both sides at the slightest sign of stickiness. Continue to dust with flour as you roll through narrower and narrower settings, if necessary; otherwise the dough will become hopelessly stuck together. By this time you will have a very long thin sheet of pliable dough that looks and even feels like a velvety chamois cloth.

4. Cut the ribbon into 6- to 12-inch lengths, 2 to 5 inches wide, unless the recipe specifies another size. Sprinkle some flour in a large baking tray and dust each length of cut lasagne on both sides with the flour. Let rest in an airy place on paper towels, white kitchen towels, or a white sheet reserved for this purpose for 1 to 2 hours before cooking, refrigerating, or freezing. Leave for 48 hours for completely dry pasta.

❖ HOMEMADE COLORED LASAGNE

There is no reason you can't make any kind of lasagne you can dream up. In gourmet pasta-making shops in Italy I've seen mushroom, parsley, tomato, asparagus, saffron, chocolate, and even blue curaçao pasta. The biggest problem with these exotic pastas is that no one seems to have thought of a good sauce to go with them. In fact, I find them a little too gimmicky. So what I present here are two traditional colored lasagne, green (spinach or other greens) and black (cuttlefish ink).

HOW TO MAKE GREEN LASAGNE (LASAGNE VERDI)

Remove the stems of 10 ounces spinach, Swiss chard, or beet greens. Wash well, several times, to remove all sand and dirt. Drain and place in a pot with the water adhering to the leaves from the last rinse. Turn the heat to high, and when the leaves have wilted, after about 4 to 5 minutes, remove from the heat, drain, and squeeze out all the water you can with the back of a spoon. Chop fine, salt lightly, and add with the eggs, salt, and olive oil in step 1 of Homemade White Flour and Egg Lasagne (pages 10–11).

HOW TO MAKE BLACK LASAGNE (LASAGNE NERE)

Black pasta is made from cuttlefish or squid ink. I recommend using the ink sac from a cuttlefish rather than a squid simply because cuttlefish, being larger, are easier to work with in a preparation that requires some knowledge of anatomy and surgeonlike skills.

Because cuttlefish are messy to work with, make sure you have a clean, uncluttered working area that is easy to clean up afterward. Lay the cuttlefish down with the tail pointing toward you. The cuttlefish has an oval-shaped bone, which functions in the same way the plasticlike quill inside a squid does. Have this bone side down, with the "stomach" side facing up toward you. Grasp the body with one hand and with the other pull out the head, tentacles, and any viscera that attach to them. Cut the tentacles off below the eyes and pop out the mouth, a kind of beak, in the center of the tentacles with your fingers. Wash under cold running water and set aside.

With a sharp 4-inch paring knife, slit the belly from top to bottom, being careful not to cut all the way through. The cuttlefish will be black with ink, but you will not yet have located the sac. Now push the bone through the slit and remove. With your hands, begin to separate the skin from the body and discard all the skin. Carefully rip the body down the middle where you have slit the cuttlefish, making sure you don't puncture the ink sac.

The ink sac is a very tiny narrow white sac with an attached tube. It is covered with a white musclelike tissue and will be flanked by eggs, if the cuttlefish is a female. Don't throw away the white egg sacs; they are a delicacy. To remove the sac, carefully grab the tube, separating it from the surrounding tissue with your fingers, and pull out both the tube and the sac.

Clean the body of the cuttlefish under cold running water, pulling off any remaining skin and any gelatinous-looking tissue. When clean, it will be completely white. Chop up the body and the tentacles to use in the Lasagne Nere con Sugo di Seppia (page 81).

Now you can begin to make the black pasta.

Holding the ink sac, point the tube downward into the middle of the well of step 1 in Homemade White Flour and Egg Lasagne (pages 10–11), in which the eggs, salt, and olive oil have already been placed. Run your fingers down the sac and tube, squeezing all the ink out. The ink is thick and very, very black. There is unlikely to be more than ½ teaspoon, but this is more than enough. Begin mixing the flour, eggs, salt, oil, and ink until you can knead the dough. It will look like a disaster as you do this, very messy and unappealing. Do not fret: not until about the eighth minute of kneading will you have a pliable, extremely black ball of dough. Now it is ready to be wrapped up and left to rest for 30 minutes to 1 hour. Continue according to the recipe. The ink sac can also be frozen for another time.

THE NEXT STEPS: PUTTING LASAGNE ON THE TABLE

Now that you have your beautifully flexible sheets of lasagne, you are ready to continue the assembly of the final dish. But whether you've put in the time and effort to make your own lasagne or are using a commercial brand, the remaining steps are important for a successful lasagne.

Cooking Homemade Lasagne

Cooking times for homemade fresh lasagne (dried 1 to 2 hours after its making) will depend on its thinness. For lasagne as thin as the thinnest setting on your rolling machine—a lasagne that will be extremely fragile — merely dunk it, one sheet at a time, into boiling, salted water and remove almost immediately with a skimmer. Do not dry.

For all other thicknesses of homemade lasagne, bring a large pot of water to a rolling, furious boil. There should be about 5 to 6 quarts of water for a pound of pasta. Salt the water abundantly, with at least 2 tablespoons, and drop the lasagne in crosswise, one at a time, so the water temperature doesn't drop too much below a boil. This method of putting the sheets of lasagne into the cooking water to form crosses so they won't stick together is referred to in Naples with the slang expression *cuntrario e scuntrario,* meeting contrariwise. Push, don't stir, the lasagne around in the pot.

It is completely useless to pour oil into the pot of water while the lasagne is cooking to prevent sticking. Oil separates from water and floats to the top, accomplishing nothing. Since cooking times for pasta vary, you need to keep your eye on the lasagne, but 1 to 2 minutes should be enough for fresh lasagne that has been dried about 2 hours. Drain immediately and return the steaming lasagne to the pot. Cover with cold water if preparing a baked dish; otherwise, serve with the sauce you've chosen. This process of submerging in cold water will stop the lasagne from cooking and will lubricate the sheets of lasagne so they don't stick together. You can leave the lasagne in the cold water until needed. If some lasagne have stuck together, you should be able to peel them apart.

You can skip this boiling step for homemade lasagne entirely if your recipe has enough sauce to cook the lasagne during baking, in the same way that "instant" lasagne gets cooked (see below).

Cooking Commercial Lasagne

Using commercial lasagne is a healthy, natural, and easy way of preparing baked and free-form lasagne recipes. Commercially made lasagne is made with durum wheat and water mostly but is also available made with eggs.

I believe the best-tasting and most convenient commercially made lasagne products for both baked and free-form lasagne are the imported "instant" lasagne. This no-boil lasagne requires no precooking when used in baked dishes. But it also has a better taste and texture than our domestic products when used for free-form lasagne recipes. For such recipes, you boil the lasagne in the usual manner, but since there are no cooking times provided, you will have to check for doneness after 4 or 5 minutes.

The Barilla company of Parma, Italy's largest pasta seller, makes a wavy lasagne sheet that requires no precooking. The Mennuci company of Lucca also offers a wavy lasagne that needs no precooking; it comes with two aluminum pans. The Delverde company markets its product as "I Primissimi — Instant Lasagne." These eighteen sheets of 9 × 8-inch "instant" microwavable wavy lasagne are packaged with three aluminum baking pans. All these products are imported and are becoming more widely available.

The one American-made instant lasagne that I know of, and it is very good, is Pasta

DeFino, made by Shade Pasta of Fremont, Nebraska. Ask your supermarket manager to carry it, if the store doesn't already.

The method of cooking commercially made lasagne is the same as for homemade lasagne, except for the time. Follow the directions on the package but remember that some recipes in this book call for half-cooked lasagne and others for al dente. Since no recipe calls for more than 1 pound of lasagne, you will need 5 to 6 quarts of furiously boiling water. Abundantly salt the water and add the lasagne crosswise, one sheet at a time (adding all the sheets at once will lower the water temperature too much). As the lasagne softens, push it about to avoid sticking.

Lasagne is the only pasta product that gets rinsed when it is drained. Place the cooked lasagne in a bowl or pot of cold water until needed; this will prevent it from sticking.

Layering and Baking

When you are ready to assemble the lasagne, lay several folds of paper towels or white kitchen towels on a work surface and damp-dry the lasagne sheets before they go into the baking pan, unless the recipe calls for you to do otherwise. Do not dry very thin lasagne — it is too fragile. If you choose not to dry the lasagne — and this applies to both homemade and commercial lasagne — it will not be disastrous, but your lasagne may turn out to be watery if your sauce is already thin. By all means don't bother drying if you find that it's too laborious; just drain the lasagne well in a colander and remember to compensate with the sauce — make it thicker. Also remember that fresh mozzarella will give off water too. After baking you can always spoon off excess water or even fat if you have used too much. In any case, a second baking or microwaving usually takes care of the problem of excess moisture.

Since this book is for home cooks preparing lasagne for family and close friends, I recommend you follow my practice and use disposable square aluminum cake pans. These pans are usually either $9 \times 9 \times 2$ inches or $8 \times 8 \times 1\frac{1}{2}$ inches. Most of the recipes assume this square pan, but you can also use the approximately $9 \times 12 \times 2$-inch aluminum "lasagna" pan. Some stores sell 4-inch-deep lasagne pans.

I prefer the square pans since they stack better in my freezer and don't waste as much room as the rectangular pans if I'm storing them half-full. I usually opt for the 2-inch-deep pans because I can fit in six layers of lasagne if I want. But since you might be using a different-size pan, as I sometimes do, here are the equivalents: each recipe yields enough for at least one $9 \times 9 \times 2$-inch pan, layered a bit over the brim (it will settle in the baking); two square pans — 8-inch or 9-inch — layered a bit more modestly; or one $11\frac{3}{4} \times 9\frac{1}{4} \times 1\frac{1}{2}$-inch lasagne pan. If you use a 4-inch-deep pan, you will need to double the recipe.

In any case, because of the variety of pans and the variety of lasagne and ingredients, you'll need to learn to estimate by sight the amount of sauces, mixtures, cheeses, or other ingredients you have and how to layer so that you end up with between four and six layers of lasagne. Many people like multiple layers, sometimes up to ten. If you layer this much lasagne, be sure to make the layers of other ingredients very meager and to use only thin homemade lasagne (or the equally thin instant) and a deep (4 inches at least) baking pan. Ten layers of commercial lasagne will be too thick and will make your dish pasty. Most of the recipes that feature multiple layers of lasagne, such as Lasagne Verdi al Forno (page 53), require that you use thin homemade lasagne, which will be separated by mere films of sauce.

Grease the lasagne pan lightly but thoroughly with butter or oil before you begin layering, making sure that the bottom and sides of the pan are completely greased. Some cooks spread a thin film of sauce on the bottom of the pan too before layering. It's OK to let the sheets of lasagne overlap.

If you have run out of sauce for the top layer of lasagne, use any tomato sauce or mix several tablespoons of tomato paste with water and coat the top. If you need béchamel for the final layer, you can make an emergency white sauce: melt 1 tablespoon unsalted butter in a saucepan, blend in 1 tablespoon all-purpose bleached or unbleached flour, add salt and pepper, whisk in ½ cup milk, and cook until thickened.

After the lasagne is layered, I cover the baking pan with a piece of aluminum foil, sealing it tightly around the edges but leaving the center tented — so that nothing sticks to it — before baking. You could also leave the pan loosely covered. If you leave the pan uncovered, the edges of the lasagne will become crispy brown. Personally, I do not care for crispy lasagne.

If the particular recipe you are making is watery or you expect it to become watery (from fresh mozzarella on top, for instance), then leave the pan uncovered for a portion of the baking time or spoon out liquid after cutting the lasagne into portions. Some recipes, especially those where the lasagne is topped with béchamel sauce or bread crumbs, are improved by leaving the baking pan uncovered. The béchamel becomes flecked with brown spots and looks very inviting, as does the golden bread-crumb crust.

Be sure to put the aluminum pans on a baking tray before placing in the oven.

Rebaking

Baked lasagne miraculously improves upon rebaking. The flavors form their final melding, and excess water is absorbed. So much better does lasagne taste after rebaking that I do not instruct you to rebake in the recipe — I assume you will do so. Be aware, though, that if your lasagne is already lacking in liquid, a rebaking might make it too dry. To avoid that problem, make sure your original sauce is abundant or spread a thin layer of tomato sauce over the top of a baked lasagne.

To rebake, the baked lasagne should be completely cool. Rebake later the same day and either serve or let cool again before refrigerating or freezing. Or freeze, then defrost, and bake at 325°F until the center is hot, about 45 minutes.

An excellent alternative to rebaking is microwaving. Remove the lasagne from its aluminum pan and transfer to a microwavable platter. This way you don't have to worry about it drying out.

ABOUT THE RECIPES

- Every recipe (with a very few exceptions) begins with the instruction "Prepare the lasagne." This refers to one of the basic homemade lasagne recipes on pages 10–14. If you would rather use the convenient commercially made store-bought dry lasagne, you can ignore this step and continue with the rest of the preparation.
- Every recipe calls for boiling and draining (and often drying) the lasagne. This step can also be ignored if you are using instant lasagne and if you are not inclined to dry the lasagne (but see my comment on page 15).
- Every recipe calls for either 1 recipe homemade lasagne or for 1 pound, ¾ pound, or ½ pound of commercial lasagne. My homemade lasagne dough recipes yield between 1 and 1½ pounds. The weight varies depending on the size of the eggs and/or the amount of water you use and on how long you dry the pasta. This means that you may have more lasagne than you will need for the recipe.

But don't worry about that. Go ahead and cook all the lasagne, and whatever remains after the dish is assembled can be stored in the refrigerator or freezer for later use in another baked or even free-form lasagne preparation. Because making homemade lasagne involves a bit of work, I feel that it is appropriate for you to make more than you need for just one recipe.

Almost every recipe allows you to substitute commercially made lasagne. Most recipes will actually use less than the 1 pound most often called for. Again, simply save it for a later use. When storing cooked lasagne, remember to store them wet so the sheets don't stick together.

- Mozzarella cheese is used in many recipes. I uniformly call for fresh mozzarella, a product with a superior taste that is made with cow's milk or an imported — and expensive — buffalo milk. Use the commercially packaged mozzarella if you can't find fresh.
- Ricotta cheese is called for in a good number of the recipes, and you need to be aware of how to use it.

Commercially made ricotta, now widely available in low-fat and whole-milk varieties, contains preservatives that give it a long shelf life but at the expense of taste. Fresh ricotta is made from a creamy curd. In fact, ricotta is technically not a cheese but curd that has been cooked twice, hence the name, which means recooked in Italian. Usually it is a by-product of provolone cheese making. When whole-milk cow's cheese is being made, the hot whey of the milk is reheated and the solid milk parts are separated from the serum — the watery part that remains after coagulation — and skimmed off to drain. This remaining casein, a phosphoprotein of milk produced when milk is curdled by rennet, is the basis of ricotta.

Fresh ricotta is usually found in Italian groceries and will keep for three days. But you can also make it yourself — it's very easy. See the recipe on page 29.

Ricotta used for lasagne needs to be thinned with water or milk to make it creamy and easier to spread. Generally you will use about 6 to 8 tablespoons of tepid water or hot milk for each pound of commercially made ricotta and ½ cup or more for fresh ricotta. If eggs are called for in the ricotta mixture, you need not thin at all. With the addition of liquid the ricotta becomes soft. An expression in Italian alludes to the soft nature of ricotta — *un uomo di ricotta* means a spineless fellow.

- I specify Parmigiano-Reggiano cheese throughout the recipes. Although many less expensive varieties of parmesan are available, Parmigiano-Reggiano — imported from Italy, with the name stamped on the rind — is the best. Never grate Parmigiano-Reggiano until you need it. And never buy grated Parmigiano-Reggiano; always buy whole.

- Many of these lasagne dishes use meat sauces, recipes for which can be found in chapter 2 or in the individual recipes. When the recipe specifies "very lean" ground meat, that means meat that is 90 percent fat-free. If you are using any other variety of ground meat, you must fry it first to render out the fat, otherwise your sauce will be heavy, greasy, and unappetizing.

- Tomato sauce is found in many recipes. I provide what I consider a superior recipe on page 22. I often double this recipe and freeze it for later use. If you are pressed for time or not inclined to make your own, then use either your favorite store-bought brand of tomato sauce or tomato puree seasoned with a few tablespoons of your favorite brand of tomato sauce.

- Beef and chicken broth are the base for several sauces used in a number of recipes. I provide two good recipes for homemade broth, on pages 28 and 29. But if you lack the time or the inclination, by all means use bouillon cubes.

- When olive oil is specified, use either virgin or inexpensive extra-virgin, whichever you have on hand. When I call for extra-virgin olive oil, it should be high-quality. For deep-frying, use pure olive oil or pomace, which is the oil extracted from crushed olive pits.

- Anchovies are an essential seasoning in

all Italian cuisine. If you love Italian food, you may already love anchovies without knowing it, for they are the secret ingredient in many preparations. Use the better quality salted anchovies sold loose and in tins at Italian markets; otherwise you'll have to settle for the inferior anchovies sold in tiny oil-packed cans.

- An asterisk (*) denotes a meatless recipe.
- In the Italian recipe names, words in quotes are from regional dialects.
- Lasagne can be baked in a 400°F oven for 25 to 30 minutes; in a 375°F oven for 30 to 35 minutes; or in a 350°F oven for 35 to 40 minutes.
- For low-fat conversions of the recipes, see below.

Low-fat Lasagne

My recipes are authentic Italian home-cooked preparations harking back to a time when most Italians were farm folk, working hard all day, burning off the calories from their richly satisfying nourishment. Our modern, sedentary lives mean we must pay attention to our diet, either lowering fat intake or exercising or both. I personally find it more enjoyable to exercise every day than to obsess about food. Luckily, lasagne is the kind of dish where taste is not too greatly diminished by making a low-fat version. Every recipe can be transformed into a low-fat lasagne. Simply follow the suggestions for these lasagne ingredients:

BÉCHAMEL: Use low-fat margarine and skim milk instead of butter and whole milk.

BUTTER: In recipes calling for melted butter to be poured over the top of the lasagne, omit it entirely or use half the amount called for. Reduce all other amounts of butter by a third or use low-fat margarine in place of butter.

LARD: Reduce the amount of lard by half or use low-fat margarine or vegetable shortening.

MEATS: Cut off all fat before cooking or preparing. When using ground beef, veal, or pork, fry it first to render out all the fat, or use very lean meats.

MOZZARELLA: Use low-fat, part-skim mozzarella instead of fresh or whole-milk mozzarella.

OLIVE OIL: You may notice that I have a somewhat heavy hand with olive oil, but that is the way I like it. If you are trying to cut down on fats, you can simply reduce the amounts I call for by a third (for example, if I call for 3 tablespoons of olive oil, use 2 tablespoons, and so on).

PANCETTA: Reduce by half.

PROSCIUTTO: Do not reduce the amount of prosciutto called for—remember (whether it makes sense or not) that the Italian verb *improsciuttire* means to become thin.

RICOTTA: Use low-fat, part-skim ricotta instead of whole-milk fresh or commercial ricotta. Or substitute low-fat cottage cheese.

SALT PORK: Reduce by half.

2

SAUCES, STOCKS, AND MORE

 SALSA BESCIAMELLA*
Béchamel Sauce

Béchamel sauce was supposedly invented by the Marquis Louis de Béchamel, a French financier of the late seventeenth century, although it is common knowledge that the ancient Greeks made an identical white sauce. In the early eighteenth century the sauce entered Italian cuisine, where it is almost exclusively associated with various baked lasagne recipes.

Whisking constantly and incorporating the milk slowly off the heat will avoid a floury-tasting béchamel.

3 tablespoons unsalted butter
3 tablespoons all-purpose bleached or
  unbleached white flour
Salt and freshly ground white pepper
2 cups hot milk
Pinch of nutmeg (optional)

1. In a saucepan melt the butter over medium heat. Add the flour, then salt and pepper to taste, and stir constantly for 2 minutes. Slowly pour in the hot milk off the heat, whisking vigorously.

2. Once all the milk is incorporated, reduce the heat to low and simmer for 12 to 15

minutes, stirring frequently. Sprinkle in the nutmeg, if using. Taste to correct the seasoning.

Makes 2 cups

Note: The sauce should be thick and velvety. If it is too thin, add a piece of *beurre manié* (1 tablespoon unsalted butter blended with 1 tablespoon all-purpose bleached or unbleached flour). If it tastes floury, add a small amount of heavy cream. In recipes calling for a thick béchamel, start with 1½ cups milk and add 2 tablespoons *beurre manié*.

 ## SALSA DI POMODORO*

Tomato Sauce

A lasagne is only as good as your tomato sauce, many Italians would say. Because of the importance of tomato sauce in various lasagne, I think it may be worth your while to quadruple this recipe and freeze any excess.

> *2 garlic cloves, peeled and slightly crushed*
> *¼ cup olive oil*
> *1 medium onion, peeled and finely chopped*
> *2 pounds ripe plum tomatoes, peeled, seeded, and chopped*
> *6 large fresh basil leaves*
> *Salt and freshly ground black pepper*
> *1 tablespoon dried oregano (optional)*

1. Sauté the garlic in the olive oil over medium-high heat in a deep sauté pan or casserole until it begins to turn light brown. Remove and discard the garlic and add the onion. Cook the onion until translucent, about 5 to 6 minutes, stirring frequently. Add the tomatoes with their liquid, basil, and salt and pepper to taste. Cook on medium-high heat for 20 to 25 minutes, uncovered. Stir occasionally with a long wooden spoon so the bottom doesn't burn and add a small amount of water if necessary. Partially cover if the sauce splatters too much.

2. When the sauce is finished, turn the heat off, add the oregano, if using, and let it steep for 10 minutes before using or storing.

Makes 3 cups

 ## RAGÙ ALLA BOLOGNESE

Bolognese-Style Meat Sauce

This famous sauce for pasta and lasagne has now become a standard in what I call international cooking, the food of hotels all over Europe and the Middle East. I have eaten mundane Bolognese sauces in such disparate places as a train station in Lübeck, Germany, and a hotel in Luxor, Egypt. Nowhere but in its Bologna home can you find its rich flavors so prominent and inviting, and the correct method of making ragù so hotly debated.

There are basically two approaches to ragù alla bolognese. In the first, recipes are rich and complex. The second approach is simpler, closer to the original of times past. This recipe is my rich ragù, while the one on page 24 is a simpler one.

The meats need to be very lean, otherwise there will be too much fat in the sauce. If your meat is fatty, fry it separately first to render out the fat. In this recipe my instructions for "very finely chopped" ingredients means pieces that are ⅟₁₆-inch dice. Cooking the ragù is nothing compared with the time and effort involved in the chopping—but it's worth it. Because of the amount of very fine chopping required, you may want to use the food processor. If you do, pulse the processor in short bursts and check often so that you do not turn the ingredients into a mush. Process the cold cuts, the vegetables, and the meats separately.

3 tablespoons dried mushrooms
3 tablespoons unsalted butter
3 tablespoons olive oil
2 ounces pancetta, very finely chopped
1 ounce prosciutto, very finely chopped
1 ounce mortadella, very finely chopped
1 medium onion, peeled and very finely chopped
1 small garlic clove, peeled and very finely chopped
1 carrot, peeled and very finely chopped
1 celery stalk, very finely chopped
2 tablespoons very finely chopped fresh parsley
¼ pound very lean beef, very finely chopped (not ground)
¼ pound very lean pork, very finely chopped (not ground)
¼ pound very lean veal, very finely chopped (not ground)
2 chicken livers, very finely chopped
½ cup red wine
¼ cup Tomato Sauce (page 22)
1 tablespoon water
¼ cup Beef Broth (page 28)
Salt and freshly ground black pepper
Pinch of nutmeg
½ cup heavy cream

1. Soak the dried mushrooms for 30 minutes in tepid water. Drain and chop very fine. Place the butter and olive oil in a heavy saucepan and heat until the butter is melted. Sauté the pancetta, prosciutto, and mortadella over medium heat for 10 minutes, stirring occasionally.

2. Add the mushrooms, onion, garlic, carrot, celery, and parsley, and cook for 10 minutes. Add the beef, pork, veal, and chicken livers, and brown, about 10 minutes.

3. Turn up the heat and add the wine. Once the wine has evaporated, add the tomato sauce with a little of the water and the beef broth. Season with salt, pepper, and nutmeg. Cover and simmer over low heat for 2 hours. Add the cream and continue cooking for another 10 minutes.

Makes enough sauce for 1¼ pounds lasagne

A SIMPLE RAGÙ ALLA BOLOGNESE
Bolognese-Style Meat Sauce

This version of the famous ragù alla bolognese is closer to the original ragù, a simple sauce for pasta. The meats need to be very lean, otherwise the sauce will be too fatty. If you use a food processor, read the comments on page 23.

3 tablespoons unsalted butter
1 medium onion, peeled and very finely chopped
1 small garlic clove, peeled and very finely chopped
1 carrot, peeled and very finely chopped
1 celery stalk, very finely chopped
2 tablespoons very finely chopped fresh parsley
¼ pound very lean beef, very finely chopped (not ground)
¼ pound very lean veal, very finely chopped (not ground)
Salt and freshly ground black pepper
½ cup red wine
1½ cups Tomato Sauce (page 22)
1 ounce prosciutto (one ⅛-inch-thick slice), very finely chopped

1. Melt the butter in a pan and sauté the onion, garlic, carrot, celery, and parsley over medium-high heat for 6 minutes, stirring frequently. Add the beef, veal, and salt and pepper to taste. Reduce the heat to medium and cook for 7 to 8 minutes (half this time if the meat has already been cooked), stirring frequently.

2. Reduce the heat to low, pour in the wine and tomato sauce, and cook for 10 minutes, covered. Stir in the prosciutto and take off the heat. Keep covered until needed.

Makes 2½ cups

 # RAGÙ ALLA NAPOLETANA
Neapolitan-Style Meat Sauce

There are a zillion versions of this classic southern Italian ragù. This recipe is very basic, and I like it.

2 pounds beef rump or chuck, in 1 piece, as square as possible
4 ounces pancetta, half cut in thin strips, half finely chopped
2 tablespoons 'nzugna (freshly rendered pork fat) (see Note), commercial pork lard, or vegetable shortening
3 tablespoons olive oil
Salt and freshly ground black pepper
2 cups water
2 cups red wine (such as Chianti)
3 cups Tomato Sauce (page 22)
6 large fresh basil leaves

1. With the tip of a sharp knife or a larding needle, make several deep incisions around the piece of beef. Push the strips of pancetta into the incisions.

2. Prepare the 'nzugna (see Note).

3. In a casserole large enough to hold the beef snugly, place the chopped pancetta along with the 'nzugna, lard, or shortening and olive oil; turn the heat to medium. Place the beef in the casserole, salt and pepper lightly, raise the heat to medium-high, and brown, about 3 to 4 minutes a side. Pour in the water and cook, turning the beef occasionally, until the water has evaporated, about 25 minutes.

4. Pour in 1 cup of the wine and ½ cup of the tomato sauce dissolved in the remaining 1 cup wine. Stir and check the seasoning. Add the basil leaves, cover, and cook for 4 hours over very low heat.

5. Remove the beef and serve as a second course or save for another use. Strain the ragù through cheesecloth. Pour into a glass or ceramic bowl or container and cool. Leave for a few hours or overnight in the refrigerator so the fat can rise to the top. Once the layer of fat has solidified, carefully remove and discard it. Stir the remaining 2½ cups tomato sauce into the ragù. Use as called for in the lasagne recipe or freeze.

Makes 3½ to 4 cups

Note: 'Nzugna or 'nzunza is a very old dialect word in southern Italy and Sicily meaning rendered pig fat. The word actually derives from the Arabic word for impurity. It is distinguished from lard by being freshly rendered, skipping the purification process that removes the bits and

pieces. Pig fat can be bought from supermarket meat departments, or the fat can be rendered from 4 pig's tails that have been split open (ask the butcher at any good supermarket); you can also use suet. Place the tails in a baking pan and bake in a 300°F oven until you have about ½ cup liquid fat. Cool and store in a jar or freeze. If you decide to do this in a microwave oven, place the pig's tails in a large microwavable container and cover with a paper towel to avoid splatters. Microwave for a minute or two on low.

 # SUGO DI UMIDO DI MAIALE
Pork and Tomato Sauce

A rich sauce typical of Naples, Sugo di Umido di Maiale is made from a pork stew and used for preparations such as Timballo di Lasagne alla Napoletana (page 44) and Lasagne di Giovedì Grasso (page 69).

The finished sauce will contain a substantial amount of fat. In the Middle Ages this kind of sauce, with all its fat, would be a major source of calories for the poorer population, who very rarely ate meat. In this recipe I call for the removal of the fat, which is essential not to the eating but only to the flavoring of the final product, so it can be discarded after its use in the sauce. Traditionally a lasagne made with this sauce — such as Lasagne di Giovedì Grasso — is eaten as a first course, and the pork cooked in the ragù is served as a second course, or *secondo piatto,* with any remaining sauce.

4 tablespoons 'nzugna *(freshly rendered pork fat) (see page 25), commercial pork lard, or vegetable shortening*

1 pound sweet Italian sausage, punctured with a fork in several places

1 small onion, peeled and finely chopped

1 carrot, peeled and finely chopped

½ celery stalk, finely chopped

2 garlic cloves, peeled and finely chopped

2 tablespoons finely chopped fresh parsley

1 tablespoon unsalted butter

2 ounces mushrooms, cleaned and finely chopped

2 pounds pork shoulder or chop, in 1 piece

¼ pound chicken livers, finely chopped

Salt

½ teaspoon red chili pepper flakes

1 cup dry white wine

3 pounds ripe tomatoes, peeled, seeded, and chopped

1 cup water (optional)

1. Prepare the 'nzugna (page 25).

2. Melt 1 tablespoon of the 'nzugna, lard, or shortening in a casserole and brown the sausage over medium heat for 12 minutes. Remove with a slotted spoon and set aside.

3. Melt the remaining 3 tablespoons 'nzugna, lard, or shortening in the casserole along with the fat from the sausage. Heat and add the onion, carrot, celery, garlic, and parsley, and sauté 4 minutes, stirring frequently. Add the butter and mushrooms, and cook until the butter melts. Add the pork shoulder or chop and the chicken livers. Mix well, salt to taste, and

sprinkle with the red chili pepper flakes. Brown the meat over medium heat for 10 minutes.

4. Pour in the wine and cook until it is evaporated. Add the tomatoes and reserved sausage. Mix well and bring to a boil. Turn the heat to low and cook for 3 to 4 hours, uncovered. Add up to 1 cup water if the sauce gets too thick.

5. Remove the meat and serve as a second course with some of the sauce, if desired. Strain the sauce through a strainer. Push the remaining sauce through a food mill and set aside to cool. Place in the refrigerator until the fat congeals. Once the layer of fat has formed on top, remove and discard it.

Makes 6 cups

 # SUGO DI CARNE MISTA
Sardinian Mixed-Meat Sauce

This sauce of mixed meats is a typical Sardinian recipe using Vernaccia, a strong white wine made locally (and elsewhere in Italy). You can replace Vernaccia with 1 cup of any white wine mixed with 1 tablespoon dry sherry.

½ pound lean ground pork

½ pound lean ground veal

¼ cup olive oil

3 tablespoons unsalted butter

1 medium onion, peeled and finely chopped

1 cup Vernaccia or *1 cup white wine mixed with 1 tablespoon dry sherry*
1 pound ripe tomatoes, peeled, seeded, and chopped
1 garlic clove, peeled and crushed
10 large fresh basil leaves
Salt and freshly ground black pepper

1. Place the pork and veal in a frying pan and cook until brown. Drain and press out all the fat from the ground meat. Discard the fat and reserve the meat.

2. In a casserole, heat the olive oil with the butter and sauté the onion over medium heat until it is translucent, about 6 minutes. Add the pork and veal, and cook for 2 minutes, stirring.

3. Pour in the wine, raise the heat to high, and let it reduce by half. Add the tomatoes, garlic, basil, and salt and pepper to taste. Cover, reduce the heat to medium, and cook for 30 minutes, stirring occasionally.

Makes enough for Lasagne degli Sposi (page 38)

▦ PESTO ALLA GENOVESE*

The great seaport of Genoa is often associated with basil, which gave birth to pesto. Pesto is said to be of Persian origin. Today it is so popular and well known that it is sold in most supermarkets in jars.

Pesto is not time-consuming to make, so I recommend you give it a try. It takes about 12 minutes of pounding in a mortar and pestle, although you can use a food processor. The highest-quality extra-virgin olive oil is essential.

This recipe will provide you with a liquid, mildly garlicky pesto. To make it stronger, use 3/4 cup olive oil and 4 garlic cloves, if that is your taste.

1 bunch fresh basil (50 to 60 medium to large leaves), washed and thoroughly dried
2 garlic cloves, peeled
Pinch of salt
2 tablespoons pine nuts, roasted
3 tablespoons freshly grated Parmigiano-Reggiano cheese
3 tablespoons freshly grated pecorino cheese
1 cup extra-virgin olive oil

1. There should be no water on the basil leaves. Leave to dry or use a salad spinner to remove the water, then damp-dry with paper towels. Place the basil, garlic, salt, and pine nuts in a marble mortar and begin gently pushing with the pestle. As the basil begins to turn into a mush, continue to pound, pressing the leaves clinging to the sides down into the center of the mortar. Pound gently so that you make the pesto into a paste, not a liquid. Slowly add the cheeses, about a tablespoon at a time every minute, and continue pounding. You should be pounding for about 9 to 12 minutes. If you use a food processor, pulse in short bursts.

2. Once the pesto is a thick paste, scrape it into a large, deep, heavy ceramic bowl and slowly begin to pour in the olive oil, stirring constantly with the back of a wooden spoon or continuing to use the pestle.

Makes 1½ cups, enough for 1½ pounds lasagne

Note: Pesto is traditionally tossed with trenette, a flat pasta about ¼ inch thick. There is an entire family of these flat pastas; from narrowest to widest, they are: bavettine, bavette, linguine fini, lingue di passeri, linguine, fettuccine, fettucelle, fettucce, trenettine, trenette, tagliarini, tagliolini, tagliolette, tagliatelle, pappardelle, lasagnette, and lasagne. Sometimes a mere millimeter separates one from another, and some are the same pasta. Each region may have its own dialect name for each of these too. Pesto also finds its way into minestrone and of course lasagne.

BRODO DI CARNE
Beef Broth

Italian beef broth is not as strong as a French *fond de boeuf,* since the meat is not browned before going into the stockpot to simmer. This recipe is a good broth that can be used in the recipes or frozen for another time.

4 pounds cracked beef marrow, shin- and/or
   shank bones, with meat
1 large onion, peeled and cut into eighths
4 plum tomatoes, cut in half
2 celery stalks, cut up
10 black peppercorns

1 bouquet garni (3 parsley sprigs, 1 fresh thyme
   sprig, 2 fresh sage leaves, and 1 bay leaf tied
   together in cheesecloth)
Salt and freshly ground black pepper

1. Put all the ingredients except the salt and pepper into a stockpot with 4 quarts cold water and bring to a boil, then reduce to a simmer. Skim the surface of foam. Partially cover and simmer on a very low heat for no less than 6 hours.

2. Pour the broth through a strainer and discard all the bones, meat, vegetables, and bouquet garni. Line the strainer with cheesecloth and pour the broth through again. Season to taste with salt and pepper.

3. To degrease the broth, let it rest until the fat congeals on top and can be lifted off. The broth can be frozen until needed.

Makes 2 to 3 quarts

BRODO DI POLLO
Chicken Broth

This is a flavorful broth and a good base for other sauces.

8 pounds chicken bones, with meat
2 carrots, sliced
3 celery stalks, with leaves, sliced
1 large onion, peeled and cut into eighths

10 black peppercorns
1 bouquet garni (6 parsley sprigs, 6 fresh thyme
    sprigs, 6 marjoram sprigs, 2 fresh sage leaves,
    and 1 bay leaf tied together in cheesecloth)
2 cups white wine
Salt and freshly ground black pepper

1. Put all the ingredients in a stockpot with
5 quarts cold water and bring to a boil. Reduce
the heat to a simmer and skim off the foam.
Partially cover and simmer over very low heat
for 6 hours.

2. Pour the broth through a strainer and
discard all the bones, meat, vegetables, and
bouquet garni. Line the strainer with cheesecloth and pour the broth through again. Season to taste with salt and pepper.

3. To degrease the broth, let it rest until the
fat congeals on top and can be lifted off. The
broth can be frozen until needed.

Makes 3 to 4 quarts

▦ FRESH HOMEMADE RICOTTA

If you are unable to find goat milk, increase
the amount of whole cow's milk to 4½ quarts.
Technically, this recipe is not ricotta, since it is
not being cooked twice, but the taste is nearly
identical.

4 quarts whole cow's milk
2 cups goat milk
2 cups heavy cream (not ultrapasteurized)
5 tablespoons freshly squeezed lemon juice

1. Pour the cow's milk, goat milk, cream, and
lemon juice into a large pot. Turn the heat to
low and bring the liquid to 175°F measuring
with a candy/frying thermometer or a meat
thermometer and making sure it does not touch
the bottom or sides of the pot. This will take
about 2 hours.

2. Line a strainer or small colander with
cheesecloth. When the curds form on the surface of the liquid, remove them with a skimmer
or slotted spoon and transfer to the strainer.
Turn the heat to medium and after 8 minutes
skim off some more curds. Turn the heat to
medium-high and skim until there are no more
curds, about 10 minutes of skimming.

3. Leave the curds to drain for 1 hour and
then transfer to a container and refrigerate.

Makes 2 pounds

3

BAKED LASAGNE

 LASAGNA

This is my family "lasagna," the one born of my mom's original concept. I usually make it on Sunday during the winter and gladly eat it all week, as will my children. To show you how personal lasagne making can become, I use wine and sugar in this recipe, additions that would probably horrify some Italian home cooks, but that's the way I like it.

1 pound commercial lasagne ricce (ruffle-edged
    lasagne)
1 tablespoon olive oil
1 pound sweet Italian sausage, crumbled
1 cup red wine
2 cups Tomato Sauce (page 22)
2 tablespoons dried oregano
1 teaspoon fresh or dried thyme
2 teaspoons fresh or dried rosemary
Salt and freshly ground black pepper
½ teaspoon fennel seed
1 tablespoon sugar or to taste
2 eggs
¾ cup freshly grated Parmigiano-Reggiano
    cheese
1 pound fresh ricotta cheese (about 2 cups)
1 pound fresh mozzarella cheese, thinly sliced

1. Bring a large pot of water to a rolling boil. Salt abundantly and drop the pasta in gradually. Drain the lasagne when half-cooked and transfer to a pot of cold water until needed. Dry the lasagne before using. (Skip this step entirely if using instant lasagne.)

2. Meanwhile, heat the olive oil in a deep saucepan. Brown the sausage over medium-high heat, about 6 minutes, breaking it up further with a wooden spoon and stirring. Add the red wine and let it evaporate for 5 minutes. Pour in the tomato sauce. Add the oregano, thyme, rosemary, salt and pepper, fennel seed, and sugar, and stir. Lower the heat to medium-low and cook for 30 to 40 minutes, so the sauce is not too thick.

3. While the sauce is cooking, beat the eggs in a mixing bowl. Add the Parmigiano-Reggiano and beat in the ricotta. Salt and pepper to taste and set aside.

4. Preheat the oven to 400°F. Lightly oil a lasagne baking pan. Layer lasagne on the bottom. Spread some ricotta mixture on top. Cover with another layer of lasagne and spoon sauce over it, then layer with the mozzarella. Continue in this order, finishing with a layer each of lasagne and mozzarella and then a few tablespoons of the remaining sauce.

5. Cover with a tented piece of aluminum foil and bake for 35 minutes. Remove and let the lasagna come to room temperature. Serve later or the next day by reheating in a 325°F oven for 45 minutes.

Serves 6

 # LASAGNE ALLA FERRARESE
Ferrara-Style Lasagne

Simply called *lasagne al forno*, oven-baked lasagne, this many-layered dish from Ferrara, in Emilia-Romagna, is interspersed with a film of béchamel and a light ladling of sauce.

Some people also sprinkle nuts into the sauce. The prosciutto can be omitted and a pinch of nutmeg added.

1 recipe Homemade White Flour and Egg Lasagne (page 10) or 1 pound commercial lasagne
1 recipe Béchamel Sauce (page 21)
8 tablespoons unsalted butter
¾ pound ground beef chuck
3 tablespoons tomato paste
3 cups Beef Broth (page 28)
1 onion, peeled and finely chopped
1 carrot, peeled and finely chopped
½ celery stalk, chopped
4 ounces prosciutto, with fat, chopped
½ cup white wine
Salt and freshly ground black pepper
1 cup freshly grated Parmigiano-Reggiano cheese

1. Prepare the lasagne.
2. Prepare the béchamel sauce.
3. In a sauté pan, melt 1 tablespoon of the

butter and brown the beef. Drain all the fat and reserve the beef. Dissolve the tomato paste in the beef broth.

4. Melt 4 tablespoons of the butter in a casserole and sauté the onion, carrot, celery, and prosciutto over medium heat for 10 minutes. Add the beef to the casserole and mix well. Turn the heat to high and pour in the wine. When the wine has evaporated, after about 2 to 3 minutes, pour in 2 cups of the beef broth, lower the heat to medium-low, add salt and pepper to taste, cover the casserole, and simmer for 1¾ hours, moistening the sauce as necessary with the remaining broth. Remove the cover and bring to a boil for about 5 minutes to reduce any excess liquid. Set aside.

5. Bring a large pot of water to a rolling boil. Salt abundantly and drop the pasta in gradually. Drain the lasagne when al dente and transfer to a pot of cold water until needed. Dry the lasagne before using. (Skip this step entirely if using instant lasagne.)

6. Preheat the oven to 400°F. Butter a lasagne baking pan with 1 tablespoon of the butter and cover the bottom with a layer of lasagne. Spread a film of béchamel, then add some meat sauce, and sprinkle on some Parmigiano-Reggiano. Continue layering in this order, finishing with a layer of lasagne. Dot the top with small slivers of the remaining butter. Cover with a tented piece of aluminum foil and bake for 25 to 30 minutes. Spoon off any excess liquid before cooling, serving, or freezing.

Serves 6 to 8

 # LASAGNE ALL'ABRUZZESE
Abruzzi-Style Lasagne

This lasagne from Abruzzi, a mountainous province in central Italy with an Adriatic coast, is stuffed with a rich meat sauce and hard-boiled eggs and finished with a drizzle of melted butter before going into the oven. Traditionally it is made with scamorza di Rivisondoli, but it will work just as well with fresh mozzarella. Instead of pancetta, some cooks use prosciutto fat. Not many Abruzzi cooks take the time any longer to make the *polpettine di vitello,* the little veal meatballs, incorporating the meat directly into the sauce instead, but I think it is an elegant touch.

> 1 recipe Homemade White Flour and Egg
>   Lasagne (page 10) or 1 pound commercial
>   lasagne
> 6 tablespoons olive oil
> 4 ounces very finely chopped pancetta or pro-
>   sciutto fat
> 1 medium onion, peeled and very finely chopped
> ½ pound very lean ground beef
> 1 cup white wine
> 2 cups tomato puree
> 2 tablespoons tomato paste
> ¼ cup water
> Salt and freshly ground black pepper
> ¾ pound lean ground veal

1 cup freshly grated pecorino or Parmigiano-
*   Reggiano cheese*
5 large eggs, 3 hard-boiled, shelled, and sliced
8 tablespoons unsalted butter
¾ pound sliced scamorza or fresh mozzarella
*   cheese*

1. Prepare the lasagne.

2. In a casserole, heat 4 tablespoons of the olive oil over medium heat and sauté the pancetta or prosciutto fat and onion until soft, about 12 minutes, stirring occasionally. Add the ground beef and wine, breaking up the beef with a fork or wooden spoon. Raise the heat to high and cook until the wine is nearly evaporated. Reduce to low and pour in the tomato puree, tomato paste, water, and salt and pepper to taste. Stir, cover, and cook over medium-low heat for 1½ hours, adding some water if necessary.

3. Meanwhile, knead the ground veal, 3 tablespoons of the pecorino or Parmigiano-Reggiano, 1 egg yolk, and salt and pepper to taste in a mixing bowl. With wet hands, so the meat doesn't stick, form into balls the size of a cherry.

4. Melt 3 tablespoons of the butter with the remaining 2 tablespoons olive oil in a sauté pan and brown the meatballs over medium heat for about 12 minutes, shaking the pan occasionally. Remove with a slotted spoon and add to the meat sauce after it has cooked for 45 minutes.

5. In a small bowl, mix 1 egg and ½ cup of the pecorino or Parmigiano-Reggiano. After the meat sauce has cooked for 1½ hours in total, turn off the heat under it and slowly add the egg-and-cheese mixture, stirring constantly.

6. Bring a large pot of water to a rolling boil. Salt abundantly and drop the pasta in gradually. Drain the lasagne when half-cooked and transfer to a pot of cold water until needed. Dry the lasagne before using. (Skip this step entirely if using instant lasagne.)

7. Butter a lasagne baking pan with 1 tablespoon butter. Cover the bottom with lasagne. Cover with some meat sauce and meatballs, a few slices of hard-boiled egg, and the scamorza or fresh mozzarella. Continue in this order, ending with a layer of lasagne and some sauce.

8. Preheat the oven to 350°F. Melt the remaining butter, mix with the remaining pecorino or Parmigiano-Reggiano, and pour over the top of the lasagne. Cover with a tented piece of aluminum foil and bake for 35 minutes.

Serves 6 to 8

LASAGNE DI SAN FREDIANO

Tuscan-Style Lasagne from San Frediano

This lasagne from Tuscany uses both white and green pasta and is topped with a golden baked béchamel sauce.

1 recipe Homemade White Flour and Egg
    Lasagne (page 10) or ½ pound commercial
    lasagne
1 recipe Green Lasagne (page 13) or ½ pound
    commercial spinach lasagne
1 recipe Béchamel Sauce (page 21)
1 tablespoon olive oil
8 tablespoons unsalted butter
1 medium onion, peeled and finely chopped
1 garlic clove, peeled and finely chopped
1 pound fresh porcini, portobello, or oyster
    mushrooms, cleaned and sliced
½ cup white wine
½ cup Beef Broth (page 28)
¼ pound prosciutto, with fat, cut into thin strips
¾ pound ground veal
Salt and freshly ground black pepper
1½ cups freshly grated Parmigiano-Reggiano
    cheese

1. Prepare the lasagne.
2. Prepare the béchamel sauce.

3. In a casserole, heat the olive oil with 2 tablespoons of the butter. Once the butter has melted, sauté the onion and garlic over medium heat until the onion is translucent, about 6 minutes, stirring frequently so the garlic doesn't burn. Raise the heat to high, add the mushrooms, and mix well. Pour in the wine and let it evaporate, about 3 to 4 minutes. Reduce the heat to medium and add the beef broth. Cook for 15 minutes. Set aside.

4. In a large sauté pan, melt 2 tablespoons of the butter and sauté the prosciutto for 10 minutes over medium heat. Add the veal and brown, about 4 minutes, breaking the meat up with a wooden spoon. Salt and pepper to taste, being careful with the salt, since the prosciutto is salty. When the mushrooms are done cooking, transfer the veal mixture to the mushroom casserole and cook for 15 minutes.

5. Bring a large pot of water to a rolling boil. Salt abundantly and drop the pasta in gradually. Drain when half-cooked and transfer to a pot of cold water until needed. Dry the lasagne before using. (Skip this step entirely if using instant lasagne.)

6. Preheat the oven to 400°F. Butter a lasagne baking pan with 1 tablespoon of the butter and cover the bottom with white lasagne. Spoon some sauce over the lasagne and cover the sauce with a sprinkling of Parmigiano-Reggiano (reserve ½ cup of the Parmigiano-Reggiano for the final layer) and a layer of green lasagne. Continue in this order, finishing with a layer of green lasagne. Cover with the béchamel sauce (layering up to ¼ inch thick

and reserving the rest, if any), sprinkle on the remaining Parmigiano-Reggiano, and dot with the remaining butter. Bake for 25 to 30 minutes, until the top is speckled brown.

Serves 6

LASAGNE PASTICCIATE

Golden-Crusted Lasagne with Ragù and Béchamel Sauce

The Italian name of this dish usually refers to lasagne from Emilia-Romagna, Lombardy, or the Piedmont combining meat ragù and béchamel sauce and topped with bread crumbs that are baked golden. Some cooks add chopped chicken giblets to the sauce. In Umbria they make a similar lasagne with prosciutto, fresh porcini mushrooms, and fresh white truffles added to the sauce.

1 recipe Homemade White Flour and Egg Lasagne (page 10) or 1 pound commercial lasagne
1 recipe Béchamel Sauce (page 21)
1 ounce dried mushrooms
6 tablespoons unsalted butter
6 fresh sage leaves
1 garlic clove, peeled and crushed
¾ pound ground beef
1 large egg
Salt and freshly ground black pepper
¼ pound cooked ham, chopped
½ cup dry white wine
1 cup Beef Broth (page 28)
1 cup freshly grated Parmigiano-Reggiano cheese
1 pound fresh mozzarella cheese, diced tiny
½ cup fresh bread crumbs

1. Prepare the lasagne.
2. Prepare the béchamel sauce.
3. Soak the dried mushrooms in warm water for 30 minutes. Drain, chop, and set aside. In a butter warmer, melt 4 tablespoons of the butter with the sage and garlic.
4. In a mixing bowl, knead together the ground beef, egg, salt, and pepper. Form the meat into small balls the size of a walnut. Place the meatballs in a lightly oiled frying pan and cook over medium heat until browned on all sides. Remove and set aside.
5. Melt the remaining 2 tablespoons butter in a large sauté pan and sauté the ham and mushrooms over medium heat for 10 minutes. Add the meatballs and cook for 2 minutes. Pour in the wine and when it has evaporated, after about 4 minutes, pour in the beef broth. Salt and pepper to taste. Reduce the heat to low and cook for 30 minutes, shaking the pan occasionally. Mix this sauce into the béchamel sauce. If the sauce is too liquid, reduce over medium-high heat, stirring frequently, for 8 minutes.

6. Bring a large pot of water to a rolling boil. Salt abundantly and drop the pasta in gradually. Drain the lasagne when half-cooked and transfer to a pot of cold water until needed. Dry the lasagne before using. (Skip this step entirely if using instant lasagne.)

7. Preheat the oven to 400°F. Remove the garlic and sage from the melted butter and discard; use half the butter to coat the bottom of a lasagne baking pan. Cover the bottom with a layer of lasagne, then some Parmigiano-Reggiano, mozzarella, and finally sauce. Continue in this order, finishing with sauce. Cover the sauce with the bread crumbs and drizzle with the remaining melted butter. Bake for 30 minutes or until the bread-crumb topping begins to turn a dark brown.

Serves 6

 # LASAGNE DEL BOSCHETTO

Forest-Style Lasagne

I normally don't pay attention to recipes on boxes, but this one, from a Delverde lasagne package, looked intriguing. I tried it and loved it; it is now a family favorite.

1 recipe Homemade Durum-Wheat and Water Lasagne (page 12) or 1 pound commercial lasagne

1 recipe Béchamel Sauce (page 21)
1 lamb or veal brain
¼ cup freshly squeezed lemon juice or vinegar
½ cup dried mushrooms, soaked for 30 minutes in tepid water
5 tablespoons unsalted butter
1 small onion, peeled and finely chopped
1 carrot, peeled and finely chopped
1 celery stalk, finely chopped
10 ounces ground beef
2 ounces prosciutto, chopped
Salt and freshly ground black pepper
Pinch of nutmeg
½ cup white wine
1 cup freshly grated Parmigiano-Reggiano cheese
1⅔ cups tomato puree
2 tablespoons freshly squeezed lemon juice
½ cup water

1. Prepare the lasagne.
2. Prepare the béchamel sauce.
3. Soak the brain in cold water for 30 minutes and then drain. In a large saucepan, add the lemon juice or vinegar to 1 quart cold water. Place the brain in this acidulated water. Bring to a gentle boil and simmer for 20 minutes. Drain and chop. Drain and chop the soaked mushrooms.
4. In a casserole, melt 4 tablespoons of the butter and sauté the onion, carrot, and celery over medium heat for 8 minutes, stirring occasionally. Add the ground beef, prosciutto, brain, mushrooms, salt and pepper to taste, and nutmeg. Stir well and pour in the wine, 1 tablespoon of the Parmigiano-Reggiano, and the

tomato puree, lemon juice, and water. Continue cooking for 10 minutes, stirring occasionally.

5. Bring a large pot of water to a rolling boil. Salt abundantly and drop the pasta in gradually. Drain the lasagne when half-cooked and transfer to a pot of cold water until needed. Dry the lasagne before using. (Skip this step entirely if using instant lasagne.)

6. Preheat the oven to 375°F. Grease a lasagne baking pan with the remaining butter and cover with a layer of lasagne. Add a layer of sauce and a layer of béchamel on top of that. Sprinkle with Parmigiano-Reggiano. Continue in this order, finishing with Parmigiano-Reggiano. Bake for 35 minutes.

Serves 6

LASAGNE IN FOGLIA
Leaves of Lasagne with Rich Veal Sauce

In the town of Ragusa, in the interior of Sicily, people make this "lasagne in leaves." A rich veal sauce is layered with thin leaves of lasagne and ricotta cheese, then crowned with a golden-crusted mixture of bread crumbs and pecorino and drizzled with olive oil.

1 recipe Homemade White Flour and Egg Lasagne (page 10) or 1 pound commercial lasagne

½ cup olive oil
1 pound veal shoulder, cut into small pieces
1 small onion, peeled and finely chopped
1 small carrot, peeled and finely chopped
1 celery stalk, finely chopped
3 tablespoons finely chopped fresh parsley
1 bay leaf
1 clove
½ cup red wine
2½ cups tomato puree
Salt and freshly ground pepper
¾ cup Beef Broth (page 28)
6 tablespoons water from the lasagne pot
¾ pound fresh ricotta cheese (about 1½ cups)
1½ cups freshly grated pecorino cheese
½ cup fresh bread crumbs
Extra-virgin olive oil for drizzling

1. Prepare the lasagne. Cut into 3-inch squares.

2. Heat 2 tablespoons of the olive oil in a skillet and brown the veal over high heat, about 4 to 5 minutes. Remove from the heat and set aside with its juices.

3. In a casserole, heat the remaining olive oil and sauté the onion, carrot, celery, parsley, bay leaf, and clove over medium heat for 8 minutes, stirring. Pour in the wine and cook until nearly evaporated, about 4 minutes. Add the tomato puree, reserved veal, and salt and pepper to taste. Reduce the heat to medium-low, keeping the sauce just below a gentle boil. Reduce the heat to low if it bubbles. Cook for 20 minutes, covered, stirring occasionally, adding at least ¼ cup and up to ¾ cup of the beef broth

if the sauce begins to dry out. Uncover and cook 10 minutes. Remove and discard the bay leaf (and the clove, if you can find it).

4. Bring a large pot of water to a rolling boil. Salt abundantly and drop the pasta in gradually. Drain the lasagne when al dente, saving 6 tablespoons cooking water, and transfer to a pot of cold water until needed. Dry the lasagne before using. (Skip this step entirely if using instant lasagne.)

5. Lightly oil a lasagne baking pan and cover the bottom with 2 tablespoons of the sauce, then a layer of lasagne. Mix the ricotta with the water. Spoon some ricotta over the lasagne, spreading gently with the back of the spoon. Spoon 2 or 3 ladles of sauce over the ricotta, spreading gently. Sprinkle some pecorino over the sauce (reserve 2 tablespoons of the pecorino for the topping). Continue in this order, finishing with a layer of lasagne. Mix together the remaining pecorino and the bread crumbs, and sprinkle over the top. Drizzle with olive oil.

6. Preheat the oven to 350°F. Bake until the top is golden, with some dark brown spots, about 30 to 35 minutes.

Serves 6 to 8

 # LASAGNE DEGLI SPOSI
Bridegrooms' Lasagne

Bridegrooms' lasagne — in Sardinian, *lasagnas de isposus* — is the Sardinian bachelor's last meal before the wedding. Fresh pecorino is wonderful in this preparation, although, frankly, I have never found it made in this country, even with all our local artisanal Italian-inspired cheesemakers. Perhaps we can encourage them to add it to their repertoire. In its place use pecorino Crotonese, sometimes sold as "eating" pecorino in neighborhood Italian markets. It is a soft cheese, sixty to ninety days old.

1 recipe Homemade Durum-Wheat and Water Lasagne (page 12) or 1 pound commercial lasagne
1 recipe Sugo di Carne Mista (page 26)
½ cup freshly grated pecorino cheese
½ pound thinly sliced fresh pecorino or pecorino Crotonese cheese
2 tablespoons unsalted butter, melted

1. Prepare the lasagne. Cut into strips 1¼ inches wide.

2. Prepare the Sugo di Carne Mista.

3. Bring a large pot of water to a rolling boil. Salt abundantly and drop the pasta in gradually. Drain the pasta when it is half-cooked.

(Skip this step entirely if using instant lasagne.)

4. Transfer the lasagne to the casserole with the sauce. Toss with the sauce and the grated pecorino. Transfer to an ovenproof earthenware casserole or a lasagne baking pan, leaving the lasagne as it is and not neatening it up. Cover the lasagne with the sliced pecorino. Pour the melted butter over the lasagne.

5. Preheat the oven to 400°F. Cover the lasagne with a tented piece of aluminum foil and bake for 30 minutes.

Serves 6

 # LASAGNE CON RICOTTA

Apulian-Style Lasagne with Ricotta

This rich and delicious lasagne from Apulia has ricotta as its star. For this reason I believe it is worth the effort to make your own (page 29) or at least visit an Italian market to find fresh ricotta. If you are using commercially made, store-bought ricotta (with its taste-killing preservatives), use half the amount of hot milk given below to thin it to a creamy consistency.

1 recipe Homemade Durum-Wheat and Water Lasagne (page 12) or 1 pound commercial lasagne

¼ cup olive oil
1 garlic clove, peeled and crushed
½ pound sweet Italian sausage, crumbled
½ cup red wine
4 tablespoons tomato paste
½ cup tepid water
Salt and freshly ground black pepper
12 large fresh basil leaves
½ pound fresh ricotta cheese (about 1 cup)
6 tablespoons hot milk
Olive oil for greasing the pan
1 cup freshly grated pecorino cheese
1 cup freshly grated Parmigiano-Reggiano cheese

1. Prepare the lasagne.

2. In a large sauté pan, heat the olive oil and sauté the garlic over medium heat until it begins to turn light brown. Remove and discard the garlic. Add the sausage and cook for 8 minutes, breaking it up with a wooden spoon and stirring occasionally.

3. Pour in the wine and cook until it is almost evaporated, about 12 minutes. Dilute the tomato paste with the tepid water and stir into the pan. Reduce the heat to low, add salt and pepper to taste, cover, and cook for 20 minutes, until the sauce is thick. Turn the heat off and stir in the basil.

4. Bring a large pot of water to a rolling boil. Salt abundantly and drop the pasta in gradually. Drain when half-cooked and transfer to a pot of cold water until needed. Dry the lasagne before using. (Skip this step entirely if using instant lasagne.)

5. Preheat the oven to 350°F. Stir the ricotta

and hot milk together until the mixture is smooth and creamy. Oil the lasagne baking pan and cover the bottom with a layer of lasagne. Cover with a layer of ricotta and then a sprinkle of pecorino and Parmigiano-Reggiano. Spoon some meat sauce over the grated cheese and continue in this order, finishing with a layer of lasagne. Spoon some meat sauce on top. Cover with a tented piece of aluminum foil and bake for 30 minutes.

Serves 6 to 8

 # LASAGNE AL NIDO
Ligurian-Style Pork Tenderloin and Ricotta Lasagne

Only the leanest pork tenderloin will work in this recipe from Liguria; you must control the amount of pork fat or the lasagne will be sodden. Roast the tenderloin first, then let it rest until cool and slice as thin as possible.

> *1 recipe Homemade White Flour and Egg*
> *Lasagne (page 10) or 1 pound commercial*
> *lasagne*
> *1¼ pounds boneless pork tenderloin, in 1 piece*
> *2 ounces pancetta, cut in very thin strips*
> *4 tablespoons unsalted butter*
> *¼ cup olive oil*
> *1 onion, peeled and finely chopped*
> *1 carrot, peeled and finely chopped*
> *1 celery stalk, finely chopped*
> *Salt and freshly ground black pepper*
> *¼ cup red wine (such as Chianti)*
> *1 cup Beef Broth (page 28)*
> *¾ pound fresh ricotta cheese (about 1½ cups)*
> *5 tablespoons tepid water*
> *1 cup freshly grated Parmigiano-Reggiano cheese*

1. Prepare the lasagne. Preheat the oven to 375°F.

2. With a larding needle or skewer, lard the pork tenderloin with the pancetta strips.

3. In a casserole that will hold the pork somewhat snugly, melt 3 tablespoons of the butter in the olive oil over medium heat and sauté the onion, carrot, and celery for 8 minutes, stirring occasionally.

4. Place the meat on top of the onion mixture; salt and pepper to taste. Pour the wine over the meat and place in the oven for 1 hour, using all the beef broth to keep the meat moist.

5. Push the ricotta through a strainer or sieve, or pass through a food mill, into a bowl and set aside. Mix 3 tablespoons of the ricotta with 1 tablespoon of the water and ¼ cup of the Parmigiano-Reggiano. Stir well and set aside. Mix the remaining ricotta with the remaining ¼ cup water, stir well until creamy, and set aside.

6. Remove the casserole from the oven and transfer the meat to a cutting board, letting it rest at least 1 hour.

7. Pour the pan juices and vegetables from the casserole into a food mill and push them through into a bowl or pot. Using a very sharp

slicing knife, slice the meat as thin as you can without shredding it. Don't saw the meat— just one quick, sharp slice, very thin.

8. Bring a large pot of water to a rolling boil. Salt abundantly and drop the pasta in gradually. Drain and transfer the lasagne to a pot of cold water until needed. Dry the lasagne before using. (Skip this step entirely if using instant lasagne.)

9. Raise the oven temperature to 400°F. Use the remaining butter to grease a lasagne baking pan and cover with a layer of lasagne. Layer with sliced pork tenderloin, some ricotta, some strained pan juices, and a sprinkling of Parmigiano-Reggiano. Continue in this order, finishing with a layer of lasagne. Spread the ricotta-and-Parmigiano-Reggiano mixture over the top of the lasagne. Cover the baking pan with a tented piece of aluminum foil and bake for 35 minutes. Remove from the oven and let cool a bit, then pour or spoon off excess juice or fat, if any.

Serves 6

"VINCISGRASSI"

This famous lasagne from the Marches, with its unusual name, is a rich and complex preparation of sheets of lasagne made with durum wheat, eggs, and Marsala. Each layer is interspersed with béchamel sauce, freshly grated Parmigiano-Reggiano cheese, and a sumptuous and thick sauce.

The classic explanation of the origin of the name of this fabulous lasagne is provided by the late American food writer Waverly Root in his book *The Food of Italy*. Root claimed that the dish was invented in 1799 by a chef from Macerata to honor Prince Alfred Fürst zu Windischgrätz, the commander of the Austrian occupation forces based in Ancona, and that *vincisgrassi* was a corruption of his name. The only problem with Root's explanation, uncritically duplicated by nearly every other food writer, is that Prince Windischgrätz was twelve years old at the time and hardly a commander.

A more likely explanation is that it was invented by Antonio Nebbia, whose book *Il cuoco Maceratese,* published nearly a hundred years earlier than the date proposed by Root, is held by the Wellcome Institute for the History of Medicine, in London. There he gave a recipe for *princesgrasse,* a princely preparation. In any case, every Italian dictionary will tell you that the origin of the name is unknown.

I use Marsala in making the lasagne, although *vin santo,* a strong, aromatic, sweet wine that is produced in Tuscany, Trentino, and on a smaller scale in Umbria and the Marches, could also be used. After you have assembled the lasagne, let it rest undisturbed in a refrigerator for 6 hours and bake it only once.

Commercial lasagne can be used in place of step 1 below.

2 cups durum-wheat flour
1 cup all-purpose unbleached white flour

2 large eggs

1 teaspoon salt

6 tablespoons Marsala wine

14 tablespoons unsalted butter (3 tablespoons at room temperature, 3 tablespoons melted)

1 recipe Béchamel Sauce (page 21)

2 tablespoons tomato paste

1 cup Chicken Broth (page 28) or Beef Broth (page 28)

1 medium onion, peeled and finely chopped

1 carrot, peeled and finely chopped

6 ounces prosciutto fat (or pancetta or pork fat), finely chopped

⅓ pound chicken hearts, chopped

¾ cup white wine

Salt and freshly ground black pepper

2 tablespoons milk

½ pound veal sweetbreads

½ pound veal brains

3 tablespoons freshly squeezed lemon juice or vinegar

⅓ pound chicken livers

½ cup freshly grated Parmigiano-Reggiano cheese

1. Prepare the lasagne. Combine the durum-wheat and white flour and, following the directions in step 1 for Homemade White Flour and Egg Lasagne (pages 10–11), incorporate the eggs, salt, Marsala, and 2 tablespoons of the room-temperature butter, broken into bits. Knead and roll out as in steps 2 and 3. After rolling, cut the lasagne into 4 × 12-inch strips.

2. Prepare the béchamel sauce. Dissolve the tomato paste in the chicken or beef broth.

3. Melt 6 tablespoons of the butter in a casserole and sauté the onion, carrot, and prosciutto fat over medium heat for 20 minutes, stirring frequently. Add the chicken hearts and wine, and continue cooking until the wine has reduced by three quarters, about 7 minutes. Add the tomato-paste-and-broth mixture. Lightly salt and pepper to taste and cook over low heat for 2 hours, stirring from time to time and adding the milk after about 30 minutes.

4. Meanwhile, soak the sweetbreads and brains in cold water for 30 minutes. Drain. In a large saucepan, add the lemon juice or vinegar to 1 quart of cold water. Place the sweetbreads and brains in this acidulated water. Bring to a gentle boil and simmer for 20 minutes. Drain, cool, and dice.

5. After the sauce has been cooking for 1½ hours, stir in the sweetbreads and brains. Ten minutes before the sauce is done, add the chicken livers.

6. *Follow this step only if using commercial non-instant lasagne.* Bring a large pot of water to a rolling boil. Salt abundantly and drop the pasta in gradually. Drain the lasagne when half-cooked and transfer to a pot of cold water until needed. Dry the lasagne before using.

7. With the remaining 1 tablespoon room-temperature butter, grease a lasagne baking pan. Cover the bottom with a layer of unboiled fresh homemade lasagne, commercial instant lasagne, or parboiled commercial non-instant lasagne. Spoon a light layer of béchamel sauce over the lasagne and sprinkle on some Parmigiano-Reggiano. Spoon on some meat sauce and dot with thin slivers of 1 tablespoon butter.

Lay down another layer of lasagne and continue in this order, finishing with some béchamel sauce and a sprinkling of Parmigiano-Reggiano. Dot the top with slivers of 1 tablespoon butter.

8. Cover the baking pan with plastic wrap and let it rest for 6 hours in the refrigerator.

9. Preheat the oven to 400°F. Bake for 30 minutes, uncovered. Remove and drizzle on the 3 tablespoons melted butter.

Serves 6 to 8

 # LASAGNE DI CARNEVALE ALLA NAPOLETANA

Lasagne for Carnival Time in Naples

From the region of Campania, around Naples, comes this substantial and festive dish traditionally served on Fat Thursday, the week before the end of Carnival. Carnival — from the medieval Latin *carne levare,* to remove meat — is the festival of merrymaking before the austere days of Lent.

This is an involved, complex dish, as befits a special occasion. Usually it is served as the main, single course and not as a *primo piatto,* or first course. Neapolitans use a small thin sausage called *cervellatina,* which can be replaced by any Italian sausage.

Neapolitans have many names for the different lasagne they make at carnival time: *lasagne Partenopea,* the ancient name of Naples and of the Siren of legend; *lasagne imbottite,* stuffed lasagne; *lasagne napoletane,* Neapolitan-style lasagne; *lasagne antiche,* old-style lasagne; or *lasagne pasticciate,* lasagne pie-style.

> *1 recipe Homemade Durum-Wheat and Water Lasagne (page 12) or 1 pound commercial lasagne*
> *2 cups Ragù alla Napoletana (page 24)*
> *½ pound sweet Italian sausage*
> *4 large eggs, 3 hard-boiled, shelled, and sliced*
> *¾ pound lean ground beef*
> *¼ cup finely chopped fresh parsley*
> *1 garlic clove, peeled and very finely chopped*
> *¼ cup fresh bread crumbs*
> *Salt and freshly ground black pepper*
> *2 tablespoons olive oil*
> *¾ pound fresh ricotta cheese (about 1½ cups)*
> *½ pound smoked mozzarella, provola, or scamorza cheese, thinly sliced*
> *½ cup freshly grated Parmigiano-Reggiano cheese*

1. Prepare the lasagne.

2. Prepare the Ragù alla Napoletana.

3. Boil the sausage for 20 minutes over medium-high heat. Drain and let cool. Slice thin and reserve.

4. In a mixing bowl, beat 1 egg. Add the ground beef, parsley, garlic, bread crumbs, and

salt and pepper to taste, and knead together. With cold wet hands, so the meat doesn't stick, form the meat into walnut-size balls.

5. In a sauté pan, heat the olive oil over medium heat and brown the meatballs, about 15 minutes, shaking the pan so they don't stick. Remove the meatballs with a slotted spoon and let cool for 10 minutes. Slice and reserve.

6. Push the ricotta through a strainer or sieve into a mixing bowl. Stir the ragù into the ricotta, a ladle at a time, mixing well. Set aside.

7. Bring a large pot of water to a rolling boil. Salt abundantly and drop the pasta in gradually. Drain the lasagne when half-cooked and transfer to a pot of cold water until needed. Dry the lasagne before using. (Skip this step entirely if using instant lasagne.)

8. Preheat the oven to 400°F. Spread some ragù mixture to cover the bottom of a lasagne baking pan. Cover with a layer of lasagne and then with some sliced meatballs; sliced sausage; more ragù; mozzarella, provola, or scamorza; hard-boiled eggs; and Parmigiano-Reggiano. Continue in this order, finishing with a layer of lasagne, ragù, and Parmigiano-Reggiano. Cover with a tented piece of aluminum foil and bake for 30 minutes.

Serves 6

 # TIMBALLO DI LASAGNE ALLA NAPOLETANA
Timbale of Lasagne Neapolitan-Style

In this festive preparation from Naples, the lasagne is layered in a savory piecrust and moistened with a rich tomato sauce of pork and chicken livers, ricotta and mozzarella, and slices of hard-boiled egg. This time-consuming but ultimately impressive and delicious timbale is sometimes seasoned with cinnamon, cloves, and even truffles. Some Neapolitans also make it with a thick tomato sauce flavored with beef, others with a thin sauce. It freezes well.

1 recipe Homemade Durum-Wheat and Water Lasagne (page 12) or 1 pound commercial lasagne

3 cups Sugo di Umido di Maiale (page 25), mixed with 1 six-ounce can tomato paste (and 1 tablespoon sugar, optional)

4 cups all-purpose bleached or unbleached white flour

8 tablespoons unsalted butter, softened and cut into bits

4 ounces 'nzugna (freshly rendered pork fat) (see page 25), commercial pork lard, or vegetable shortening

7 eggs, 4 hard-boiled, shelled, and sliced
3 tablespoons sugar
1 teaspoon salt
1½ cups freshly grated Parmigiano-Reggiano
   cheese
¼ pound fresh ricotta cheese (about ½ cup)
3 tablespoons water
½ to ¾ pound fresh mozzarella cheese, sliced

1. Prepare the lasagne.
2. Prepare the Sugo di Umido di Maiale.
3. Bring a large pot of water to a rolling boil. Salt abundantly and drop the pasta in gradually. Drain the lasagne when half-cooked and transfer to a pot of cold water until needed. Dry the lasagne before using. (If using instant or fresh lasagne, it too needs to be parboiled, about 3 to 4 minutes.)
4. Prepare the pie dough. Pour the flour onto a work surface and make a well. Into the well, place the butter, the *'nzugna,* lard, or shortening, and 2 eggs, sugar, and salt. Start to knead the mixture together with your fingers, adding up to ⅜ cup water if necessary. Once the dough can be formed into a ball, wrap in plastic wrap or wax paper and refrigerate for 1 hour.
5. Divide the dough into 4 sections, 2 larger than the others. Lightly flour a work surface and flatten the dough. With a rolling pin, roll each of the 4 pieces of dough out to a thickness of ¼ inch or less. Fit each of the 2 larger circles of dough into a well-greased 9-inch pie pan or straight-sided mold. Trim the edges with scissors. Roll the 2 smaller pieces of dough into flat 8- to 9-inch circles, the same size as the top of the pie pans or molds, and lay on a well-greased flat baking tray.
6. Preheat the oven to 350°F. Bake the dough until it is golden, about 25 minutes. (The flat pieces will bake quicker, in about 18 to 20 minutes.) Let the dough cool in the pans or molds and the flat pieces on a rack.
7. Place the parboiled lasagne in a large mixing bowl and stir in half the Sugo di Umido di Maiale and ½ cup of the Parmigiano-Reggiano. Toss well but gently. Set aside.
8. In a small mixing bowl, stir together ½ cup of the Parmigiano-Reggiano and the ricotta, water, and 1 egg until the mixture looks thick and creamy. Set aside.
9. Layer half of the lasagne into each pie or mold. Cover with the mozzarella, then the ricotta mixture, and finally the sliced hard-boiled eggs. Cover with the remaining lasagne and carefully pour the remaining sauce over the lasagne. Sprinkle the top with the remaining ½ cup Parmigiano-Reggiano and place in a 350°F oven for 20 minutes.
10. Remove the pies from the oven and let them rest for 5 minutes. Place the 2 flat baked circles of dough over the tops of the baked pies. Place an inverted round serving plate over the pies and flip over quickly, inverting the pies, which will slide out easily. Be careful to do this with a very good grip. Serve with remaining sauce, if any, and extra Parmigiano-Reggiano.
Serves 8

"SAGNE CHINE"

Calabrian-Style Lasagne

This famous lasagne from Calabria is a festive preparation for Easter. It is also known in Basilicata, the Salerno region of Campania, and Naples. *Sagne chine,* which is Calabrian dialect for stuffed lasagne, is packed with layers of hard-boiled eggs, slices of soft cheese, onions, mushrooms, peas, artichokes, and *polpettine* (miniature meatballs) cooked in lard.

> 1 recipe Homemade Durum-Wheat and Water
>   Lasagne (page 12) or 1 pound commercial
>   lasagne
> 2 cups Ragù alla Napoletana (page 24)
> 2 artichokes, trimmed
> 4 eggs, 1 small, and 3 large (hard-boiled,
>   shelled, and sliced)
> 6 ounces ground pork tenderloin
> ½ cup freshly grated pecorino cheese
> Salt and freshly ground black pepper
> Flour for dredging
> ¾ cup olive oil
> 1 small onion, peeled
> 1 carrot, peeled
> 1 celery stalk
> 1 bay leaf
> ½ pound fresh porcini, portobello, or oyster
>   mushrooms, cleaned and thinly sliced
> 1 cup fresh shelled or frozen peas
> ½ pound fresh provola or mozzarella cheese,
>   diced

1. Prepare the lasagne.
2. Prepare the Ragù alla Napoletana.
3. Remove the chokes of the artichokes and keep the hearts and trimmed stems in a bowl of cold acidulated water (water mixed with a little freshly squeezed lemon juice or vinegar) while you work so they do not discolor.
4. In a mixing bowl beat the small egg. Add the ground pork, 2 tablespoons pecorino, and salt and pepper to taste, and knead together with your hands. Form the meat into balls the size of a walnut with cold wet hands to keep the meat from sticking. Dredge the meatballs in the flour, shaking off any excess. Heat ½ cup of the olive oil in a pan over high heat and fry the meatballs until golden brown, about 5 minutes. Remove the meatballs with a slotted spoon to drain on paper towels. Remove the frying pan from the heat and set aside, reserving the oil. Once the meatballs have cooled for 20 minutes, slice them.
5. Chop the onion, carrot, and celery together very fine and sauté over medium heat with the bay leaf and some salt and pepper in the same frying pan in which you cooked the meatballs until the onions are soft, about 4 to 5 minutes. Reduce the heat to low and add the mushrooms and peas. Stir and check the seasoning. Cook for 10 minutes, then remove and discard the bay leaf. Set aside.
6. Meanwhile, slice the artichoke hearts and stems very thin. In a small frying pan, heat 3 tablespoons of the olive oil over medium heat and sauté the artichokes with 2 tablespoons water and some salt for 20 minutes, adding 1 table-

spoon water to the pan at a time as necessary to keep it from drying out entirely. Set aside.

7. Bring a large pot of water to a rolling boil. Salt abundantly and drop the pasta in gradually. Drain the lasagne when half-cooked and transfer to a pot of cold water until needed. Dry the lasagne before using. (Skip this step entirely if using instant lasagne.)

8. Preheat the oven to 400°F. Spread a few tablespoons of ragù on the bottom of a lasagne baking pan. Cover with a layer of lasagne, some ragù, then some mushroom sauce, meatballs, artichokes, sliced hard-boiled egg, and provola or mozzarella. Continue in this order, finishing with a layer of lasagne, some ragù, and a sprinkling of the remaining pecorino. Drizzle with the remaining 1 tablespoon olive oil, cover with a tented piece of aluminum foil, and bake for 30 minutes.

Serves 6

 # LASAGNE IMBOTTITE
Calabrian-Style Stuffed Lasagne

This is another version of "Sagne Chine" (preceding recipe) but with thin slices of pork tenderloin and pork meatballs. The sauce is a rich ragù made with dried mushrooms and peas. This recipe, which can also be referred to as *sagne chine,* is often served as a main course.

1 recipe Homemade Durum-Wheat and Water Lasagne (page 12) or 1 pound commercial lasagne
1 pound pork tenderloin
3 large eggs, 2 hard-boiled, shelled, and sliced
½ cup freshly grated pecorino cheese
Salt and freshly ground black pepper
6 tablespoons olive oil
1 small onion, peeled
½ carrot, peeled
½ celery stalk
1 ounce dried mushrooms, soaked for 30 minutes in warm water, drained, and finely chopped
¾ cup fresh shelled or frozen peas
½ cup water
2 cups Tomato Sauce (page 22)
¼ pound fresh mozzarella cheese, diced tiny

1. Prepare the lasagne.

2. Cut 6 to 8 very thin slices from the pork tenderloin and, between 2 pieces of wax paper, pound them even thinner with the side of a cleaver or mallet. Set aside. Grind the remaining pork tenderloin, including a bit of pork fat or lard so the meatballs won't be too dry.

3. In a mixing bowl, beat 1 egg and add the ground pork tenderloin, 2 tablespoons of the pecorino, and salt and pepper to taste. Knead the mixture together well with your hands. Wet your hands with cold water so the meat will not stick and form small walnut-size balls. Set aside as you finish forming the balls.

4. In a sauté pan, heat 3 tablespoons of the olive oil over medium heat and brown the meatballs, about 15 minutes, shaking often so

they don't stick. Remove the meatballs with a slotted spoon to some paper towels to drain. Let cool for 15 minutes, then slice in half. In the same pan, brown the pork slices, 1 minute per side. Remove the pan from the heat and set aside, reserving the oil.

5. Chop the onion, carrot, and celery very fine or pulse them in a food processor. In the same pan in which you cooked the meatballs, put 2 tablespoons of the olive oil and sauté the onion mixture with the mushrooms over medium heat for 6 minutes, stirring frequently. Add the peas, water, and 1 cup of the tomato sauce, scraping the bottom and sides of the pan as you stir. Reduce the heat to low and simmer for 10 minutes.

6. Bring a large pot of water to a rolling boil. Salt abundantly and drop the pasta in gradually. Drain the lasagne when half-cooked and transfer to a pot of cold water until needed. Dry the lasagne before using. (Skip this step entirely if using instant lasagne.)

7. Preheat the oven to 400°F. Lightly oil a lasagne baking pan with the remaining 1 tablespoon olive oil and cover the bottom with a layer of lasagne, 1 of the sliced hard-boiled eggs, then some mozzarella, some meatballs, all of the pork slices, some sauce, and pecorino. Continue in this order, finishing with a layer of lasagne and sauce. Spread the remaining 1 cup tomato sauce over the top and sprinkle with the remaining pecorino. Cover with a tented piece of aluminum foil and bake for 30 minutes.

Serves 6

 # LASAGNE INCASSETTATE
Embedded Lasagne

This lasagne from Ancona, the capital of the Marches, on the Adriatic, is commonly made with Gruyère cheese, although some cooks use fontina or mozzarella too. One could also add truffles to the ragù and serve it on top of some buttered and tossed lasagne.

> *1 recipe Homemade White Flour and Egg Lasagne (page 10) or 1 pound commercial lasagne*
> *1 recipe Simple Ragù alla Bolognese (page 24)*
> *6 tablespoons unsalted butter*
> *¼ pound chicken breast, chopped*
> *¼ pound chicken livers, chopped*
> *1 cup freshly grated Gruyère cheese*
> *1 cup freshly grated Parmigiano-Reggiano cheese*

1. Prepare the lasagne. Cut in 3-inch squares or 1-inch-wide strips.

2. Prepare the Simple Ragù alla Bolognese.

3. In a sauté pan, melt 3 tablespoons of the butter and sauté the chicken breast and chicken livers over medium heat for 5 minutes, stirring occasionally. Add the chicken to the Ragù alla Bolognese.

4. Bring a large pot of water to a rolling boil. Salt abundantly and drop the pasta in gradu-

ally. Drain the lasagne when half-cooked and transfer to a pot of cold water until needed. Dry the lasagne before using. (Skip this step entirely if using instant lasagne.)

5. Butter a lasagne baking pan and cover the bottom with a layer of lasagne. Mix the Gruyère and Parmigiano-Reggiano together. Melt the remaining 3 tablespoons butter. Spoon some ragù over the lasagne and sprinkle on some cheese. Continue in this order, finishing with ragù and a light sprinkling of cheese. Drizzle the melted butter over the top.

6. Preheat the oven to 375°F. Cover the baking pan with a piece of tented aluminum foil and bake for 35 minutes.

Serves 4 to 6

▦ LASAGNE PIEMONTESE

Piedmont-Style Lasagne

This lasagne, from the northwestern Italian province of Piedmont, is unique in having grated Parmigiano-Reggiano cheese blended into the lasagne dough. You could also serve it as a free-form lasagne. Although you can use any kind of mushroom, a strongly flavored variety such as a portobello accompanies the chicken livers much better and improves the taste.

1 recipe Homemade White Flour and Egg Lasagne (page 10) or 1 pound commercial lasagne
4 tablespoons freshly grated Parmigiano-Reggiano cheese
½ pound chicken livers
10 tablespoons unsalted butter (3 tablespoons melted)
¾ pound mushrooms, cleaned and thinly sliced
¼ cup dry white wine
Salt and freshly ground black pepper
2 cups Chicken Broth (page 28)
1 cup freshly grated Parmigiano-Reggiano cheese

1. Prepare the lasagne, incorporating the 4 tablespoons Parmigiano-Reggiano into the dough.

2. Soak the chicken livers in cold water for 1 hour.

3. In a casserole, melt 4 tablespoons of the butter over medium heat and sauté the mushrooms for 1 minute to coat with the butter. Pour in the wine with some salt and pepper to taste. Cook for 30 minutes, moistening the mushrooms with up to 1½ cups of the chicken broth, stirring occasionally.

4. Meanwhile, after the mushroom sauce has cooked for 15 to 20 minutes, drain the chicken livers, dry with paper towels, and chop. In a small pan, melt 3 tablespoons of the butter and sauté the chicken livers over medium heat for 10 minutes. Salt and pepper to taste. Add the chicken livers to the mushroom sauce with the

remaining ½ cup chicken broth and cook for 15 minutes.

5. Bring a large pot of water to a rolling boil. Salt abundantly and drop the pasta in gradually. Drain the lasagne when al dente and transfer to a pot of cold water until needed. Dry the lasagne before using. (Skip this step entirely if using instant lasagne.)

6. Preheat the oven to 350°F. Lightly butter a lasagne baking pan. Cover the bottom of the pan with a layer of lasagne. Spoon the mushroom sauce over the lasagne and then add a sprinkling of Parmigiano-Reggiano. Continue in this order, finishing by drizzling the melted butter over the top. Cover with a tented piece of aluminum foil and bake for 30 minutes.

Serves 4 to 6

Note: For a free-form version, cook the lasagne and then toss with 8 tablespoons unsalted butter, ¼ cup freshly grated Parmigiano-Reggiano cheese, the mushroom sauce, black pepper to taste, and a pinch of nutmeg.

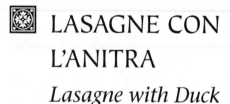

LASAGNE CON L'ANITRA

Lasagne with Duck

In this preparation familiar to duck hunters' wives in the lake regions of upper Lombardy, in northern Italy, teal, a small short-necked duck, is made into a rich lasagne. Since you will most likely be using the domestic mallard found in supermarkets, it is important to remove as much fat as possible. This recipe is adapted from one by Vincenzo Buonassisi.

> *1 recipe Homemade White Flour and Egg Lasagne (page 10) or 1 pound commercial lasagne*
> *1 duck (about 4½ pounds)*
> *1 recipe Béchamel Sauce (page 21)*
> *8 tablespoons unsalted butter*
> *2 medium onions, peeled and finely chopped*
> *1½ cups heavy cream*
> *Salt and freshly ground black pepper*
> *½ cup Marsala wine*
> *½ cup Beef Broth (page 28)*
> *1 cup freshly grated Parmigiano-Reggiano cheese*

1. Prepare the lasagne. Cut into large squares.

2. Preheat the oven to 425°F.

3. Prick the duck thoroughly over its entire body so the fat can drip out. I usually use 2 corncob holders for this purpose. Put the duck, untrussed, on a rack in a baking pan and place in the oven. Immediately reduce the heat to 350°F and roast for 1 hour. Remove the duck and when it is cool, bone it, scraping off and discarding all the fat from the meat and the skin. Cut up the duck into bite-size pieces.

4. Prepare the béchamel sauce.

5. Melt 6 tablespoons of the butter in a casserole and sauté the onions over medium heat until translucent, about 8 minutes. Add the

duck pieces to the casserole and continue cooking for 10 minutes, stirring occasionally. Add half the cream and cook for 5 minutes, stirring frequently. Pour in the remaining cream, salt and pepper to taste, and continue stirring. When the cream has reduced, after 5 minutes, pour in the Marsala and cook until the Marsala is nearly evaporated, about 8 minutes. Pour in the beef broth and cook until the sauce is thick, about 12 minutes, stirring occasionally.

6. Turn the heat off under the casserole. Remove the duck with a slotted spoon to a food processor and grind for 30 seconds. Return the ground duck to the casserole with 1 tablespoon of the butter and stir well to blend. Check the seasoning.

7. Bring a large pot of water to a rolling boil. Salt abundantly and drop the pasta in gradually. Drain the lasagne when half-cooked and transfer to a pot of cold water until needed. Dry the lasagne before using. (Skip this step entirely if using instant lasagne.)

8. Preheat the oven to 400°F. Butter a lasagne baking pan with the remaining 1 tablespoon butter and layer some lasagne to cover the bottom. Spoon some duck sauce, then some béchamel, and finally some Parmigiano-Reggiano over the lasagne. Continue in this order, finishing with béchamel and a sprinkling of Parmigiano-Reggiano. Cover with a tented piece of aluminum foil and bake for 30 minutes.

Serves 6

 # LASAGNE AL TONNO
Lasagne with Tuna

Homemade lasagne is immeasurably better than commercially made, especially in a baked lasagne as subtle as this Sicilian one made with tuna, vegetables, and tomato.

> *1 recipe Homemade Durum-Wheat and Water*
>   *Lasagne (page 12) or 1 pound commercial*
>   *lasagne*
> *⅓ cup olive oil*
> *1 medium onion, peeled and very finely chopped*
> *1 carrot, peeled and very finely chopped*
> *1 celery stalk, very finely chopped*
> *2 pounds ripe tomatoes, peeled, seeded, and*
>   *chopped*
> *½ cup water*
> *Salt and freshly ground black pepper*
> *6-ounce can tuna in olive oil, mashed*
> *¼ cup finely chopped fresh parsley*
> *Extra-virgin olive oil for drizzling*
> *½ pound fresh mozzarella cheese*
> *½ cup fresh bread crumbs*

1. Prepare the lasagne.
2. In a casserole, heat the olive oil over medium heat and sauté the onion, carrot, and celery for 8 to 10 minutes, stirring occasionally. Add the tomatoes, water, and salt and pepper to taste. Reduce the heat to medium-low and cook for 1 hour, covered, stirring occasionally.

Turn the heat off and add the tuna, with its oil, and parsley. Mix well.

3. Bring a large pot of water to a rolling boil. Salt abundantly and drop the pasta in gradually. Drain the lasagne when half-cooked and transfer to a pot of cold water until needed. Dry the lasagne before using. (Skip this step entirely if using instant lasagne.)

4. Preheat the oven to 350°F. Lightly oil a lasagne baking pan and arrange a layer of lasagne on the bottom. Ladle a small amount of tuna sauce on top, spreading it around the pan. Add another layer of lasagne and tuna sauce and continue in this manner until both are used up. Drizzle with some extra-virgin olive oil and cover with the mozzarella as the last layer. Finally, sprinkle the bread crumbs over the cheese and lightly drizzle more extra-virgin olive oil over the bread crumbs. Bake for 35 minutes, uncovered.

Serves 6

▣ LASAGNETTE E LUMACHE
Lasagnette with Snails

Call them escargots (their French name) and nearly everyone will eat snails. But this delicious recipe is perfect for both the snail lover and the slightly squeamish. It is very flavorful, with a sauce of abundant parsley, garlic, olive oil, and white wine. Lasagnette is a pasta about ¾ inch wide. The preparation is improved with almost-impossible-to-find fresh snails, although you can try ethnic Italian or Chinese stores. The dish is still great with canned snails or with mussels. If you are using either of these as a substitute, skip steps 2 and 3.

> *1 recipe Homemade White Flour and Egg Lasagne (page 10) or ¾ pound commercial lasagnette*
> *2½ pounds fresh snails, in the shell, or 48 canned snails, or 36 steamed mussels, removed from their shells*
> *½ cup olive oil*
> *1 bunch finely chopped fresh parsley, leaves only*
> *2 garlic cloves, peeled and finely chopped*
> *Salt and freshly ground black pepper*
> *1 cup white wine*
> *Freshly ground black pepper*

1. Prepare the lasagne. Cut into strips ¾ inch wide.

2. Purge the fresh snails by placing them in a bowl of cold water with 1 tablespoon baking soda for 48 hours. Continue to change the water after it is fouled until it is completely clear after 1 hour undisturbed.

3. Bring a pot of water to a boil and add the snails for 15 minutes. Drain and, with a small lobster fork or toothpick, pull the snails out.

4. In a large sauté pan, heat the olive oil and sauté the parsley and garlic over medium heat for 1 minute, stirring constantly. Add the snails, salt and pepper to taste, and reduce the heat to

medium-low. Cook for 10 minutes. Turn the heat to high, pour in the wine, and reduce by half, about 8 to 10 minutes. (If using mussels, sauté 1 minute, add 3 tablespoons wine, and cook 2 minutes.)

5. Preheat the oven to 425°F. Bring a large pot of water to a rolling boil. Salt abundantly and drop the pasta in gradually. Drain when al dente and transfer to the sauté pan. Toss well with the snail sauce; then transfer to a baking pan and bake for 12 minutes. Remove from the oven, sprinkle on some pepper, and serve.

Serves 4 to 6

 # LASAGNE VERDI AL FORNO
Oven-Baked Green Lasagne

This is the classic lasagne of Bologna, in Emilia-Romagna. It requires some work, as you can see from the complex ragù and béchamel sauce called for, not to mention homemade spinach lasagne, which I recommend highly over the commercial variety in this special preparation.

The lasagne is best if all the layers are thin — so use homemade or white instant lasagne. The homemade lasagne should be rolled out so that it could be called translucent. The layers of ragù and béchamel should be mere films. This lasagne of Emilia-Romagna is in distinct contrast to the lasagne most

Americans are familiar with, which was inherited from Italian-Americans, who are in the main from southern Italy. Here everything is light and ephemeral.

1 recipe Green Lasagne (page 13) or 1 pound
  commercial spinach lasagne
1 recipe Béchamel Sauce (page 21)
1 recipe Ragù alla Bolognese (page 22 or 24)
4 tablespoons unsalted butter
1 cup freshly grated Parmigiano-Reggiano
  cheese

1. Prepare the lasagne.
2. Prepare the béchamel sauce.
3. Prepare the rich or Simple Ragù alla Bolognese.
4. Bring a large pot of water to a rolling boil. Salt abundantly and drop the pasta in gradually. Drain the lasagne when half-cooked and transfer to a pot of cold water until needed. Dry the lasagne before using. (Skip this step entirely if using instant lasagne.)
5. Butter a lasagne baking pan and cover the bottom with lasagne. Cover the lasagne with some Ragù alla Bolognese, then some béchamel. Sprinkle some Parmigiano-Reggiano over the béchamel. Continue in this order, finishing with a layer of lasagne and a thin coat of béchamel. Sprinkle the remaining Parmigiano-Reggiano on top.
6. Preheat the oven to 400°F. Melt the remaining butter and drizzle over the top. Bake for 30 minutes, uncovered.

Serves 6

LASAGNE VERDI CASALINGHE CON SUGO DI CARNE

Home-Style Green Lasagne with Meat Sauce

This typical family recipe from Emilia-Romagna is a rough-and-ready lasagne, nothing fancy, just good, solid, rich tastes that would satisfy an Italian family home from work and school. Every family will do something different — some might add sausage, others peas, or perhaps other cheeses. If you are using ground meat that is less than 90 percent lean, cook it separately and discard the excess fat. Since the prosciutto is salty, taste the meat sauce before adding salt to it.

1 recipe Green Lasagne (page 13) or 1 pound commercial spinach lasagne
1 recipe Béchamel Sauce (page 21)
8 tablespoons unsalted butter (3 tablespoons melted)
1 small onion, peeled and very finely chopped
½ carrot, peeled and very finely chopped
1 celery stalk, very finely chopped
¼ pound very lean ground beef
Freshly ground black pepper
1 cup Beef Broth (page 28)

5 ounces finely diced prosciutto
1 cup freshly grated Parmigiano-Reggiano cheese

1. Prepare the lasagne.
2. Prepare the béchamel sauce.
3. Melt 4 tablespoons of the butter in a casserole and sauté the onion, carrot, and celery over medium heat for 10 to 12 minutes, stirring frequently. Add the beef and pepper to taste, and continue cooking, adding small amounts of the beef broth a little at a time until you have used it all up, cooking for 15 to 20 minutes. Add the prosciutto and continue cooking over a very low heat until needed.
4. Bring a large pot of water to a rolling boil. Salt abundantly and drop the pasta in gradually. Drain the lasagne when half-cooked and transfer to a pot of cold water until needed. Dry the lasagne before using. (Skip this step entirely if using instant lasagne.)
5. Preheat the oven to 400°F. Butter a lasagne baking pan with 1 tablespoon of the butter and layer on some lasagne to cover the bottom. Then add some meat sauce, béchamel sauce, and Parmigiano-Reggiano. The last layer should be lasagne topped with béchamel. Sprinkle the top with Parmigiano-Reggiano and pour the melted butter on top. Cover with a tented piece of aluminum foil and bake for 30 minutes.
Serves 6

LASAGNE VERDI PASTICCIATE ALLA MODENESE

Green Lasagne Modena-Style

This spinach lasagne from Modena, in Emilia-Romagna, is a variation on Lasagne Verdi Casalinghe con Sugo di Carne (preceding recipe). It is interspersed with a drizzling of melted butter and topped with a béchamel sauce that becomes golden-flecked in baking.

> *1 recipe Green Lasagne (page 13) or 1 pound commercial spinach lasagne*
> *½ recipe Béchamel Sauce (page 21)*
> *12 tablespoons unsalted butter (8 tablespoons melted)*
> *1 small onion, peeled and very finely chopped*
> *½ carrot, peeled and very finely chopped*
> *1 celery stalk, very finely chopped*
> *¼ pound very lean ground beef*
> *Freshly ground black pepper*
> *1 cup Beef Broth (page 28)*
> *5 ounces finely diced prosciutto*
> *1 cup freshly grated Parmigiano-Reggiano cheese*

1. Prepare the lasagne. Cut into 1-inch strips or 3-inch squares. Dry for 1 to 2 hours.

2. Prepare the béchamel sauce.

3. Melt 4 tablespoons of the butter in a casserole and sauté the onion, carrot, and celery over medium heat for 12 minutes, stirring frequently. Add the beef and pepper to taste, and continue cooking, adding small amounts of the beef broth until you have used it all up, for 20 minutes. Add the prosciutto, reduce the heat to low, and continue cooking over very low heat until needed.

4. Bring a large pot of water to a rolling boil. Salt abundantly and drop the pasta in gradually. Drain the lasagne when half-cooked and transfer to a pot of cold water until needed. Dry the lasagne before using. (Skip this step entirely if using instant lasagne.)

5. Preheat the oven to 400°F. Butter a lasagne baking pan and layer the lasagne. Spoon the meat sauce over the lasagne and sprinkle on some Parmigiano-Reggiano. Continue in this order, drizzling melted butter over each layer of lasagne, using up to three quarters of the total, and finish with a layer of lasagne. Over the top layer of lasagne spoon the béchamel sauce and sprinkle the remaining Parmigiano-Reggiano. Drizzle the remaining melted butter over the top. Bake for 30 minutes, uncovered.

Serves 6

LASAGNE VERDI ALLA RICOTTA

Green Lasagne

with Ricotta

This is a home-style family lasagne from Emilia-Romagna. There are many slight variations on this kind of lasagne verdi, but this is one I think especially perfect for a cool autumn Saturday when you could also make Fresh Homemade Ricotta (page 29).

1 recipe Green Lasagne (page 13) or 1 pound commercial spinach lasagne
1 cup Tomato Sauce (page 22)
4 tablespoons unsalted butter (2 tablespoons melted)
3 tablespoons olive oil
¼ pound lean ground beef
¼ pound lean ground pork
¼ pound cooked ham, finely chopped
1 ounce mortadella, finely chopped
1 medium onion, peeled and finely chopped
1 small carrot, peeled and finely chopped
1 celery stalk, finely chopped
Salt and freshly ground black pepper
½ cup red wine
¾ pound fresh ricotta cheese (about 1½ cups)
6 tablespoons hot milk
Pinch of nutmeg

1. Prepare the lasagne.
2. Prepare the tomato sauce.
3. In a large sauté pan, melt 2 tablespoons of the butter with the olive oil and sauté the beef, pork, ham, mortadella, onion, carrot, and celery over medium heat for 15 minutes, stirring occasionally. Salt and pepper to taste and pour in the wine. Let the wine evaporate, about 6 to 7 minutes, and add the tomato sauce. Reduce the heat to low and simmer until thick, about 5 to 10 minutes.
4. In a mixing bowl, beat the ricotta with the hot milk, nutmeg, and salt and pepper to taste.
5. Bring a large pot of water to a rolling boil. Salt abundantly and drop the pasta in gradually. Drain the lasagne when half-cooked and transfer to a pot of cold water until needed. Dry the lasagne before using. (Skip this step entirely if using instant lasagne.)
6. Preheat the oven to 400°F. Butter a lasagne baking pan and layer the bottom with lasagne. Cover the lasagne with some of the ricotta mixture and then some sauce. Continue in this order, finishing with sauce. Pour the melted butter over the top. Cover with a tented piece of aluminum foil and bake for 30 minutes.

Serves 4 to 6

LASAGNE VERDI CON CERVELLA FRITTA

Green Lasagne with Golden-Crusted Brain Patties

This lasagne from northern Italy is one I was reluctant to say too much about to my guests one evening because I knew there were some finicky eaters. I didn't mention the brains, and the positive response was extraordinary. This is the perfect dish with which to introduce novices to the delicious taste of brains.

1 recipe Green Lasagne (page 13) or 1 pound
  commercial spinach lasagne
1 pound veal brains
¼ cup freshly squeezed lemon juice or vinegar
Flour for dredging
2 eggs, beaten
Fresh bread crumbs for dredging
3 tablespoons unsalted butter
¼ cup olive oil
1 cup tomato puree
4 fresh sage leaves
Salt and freshly ground black pepper
1 cup cleaned and thinly sliced mushrooms
½ cup white wine

1. Prepare the lasagne. Cut into 1½-inch-wide strips. Dry for 1 hour.

2. While the lasagne is drying, soak the brains in cold water for 30 minutes and then drain. In a large saucepan, add the lemon juice or vinegar to 1 quart cold water. Place the brains in this acidulated water. Bring to a gentle boil and simmer for 20 minutes.

3. Drain the brains and cut into quarters. Dredge in flour. Dip in the beaten eggs and dredge in the bread crumbs. Set aside in the refrigerator for 30 minutes.

4. In a large sauté pan, melt the butter with the olive oil over high heat. When the oil is hot but not burning the butter, add the brains and fry until golden brown, about 4 minutes a side. Remove with a slotted spoon and drain on paper towels. Remove the sauté pan from the burner and reduce the heat to low.

5. Pour the tomato puree into the same sauté pan in which you cooked the brains, once it has cooled sufficiently. Add the sage, salt and pepper to taste, and cook over low heat for 10 minutes, stirring frequently. Add the mushrooms and wine, and cook for 10 minutes.

6. Preheat the oven to 425°F. Bring a large pot of water to a rolling boil. Salt abundantly and drop the pasta in gradually. Drain the lasagne when al dente and transfer to an oven-proof serving platter. Pour the sauce over the lasagne and toss gently. Arrange the reserved fried brains over the lasagne. Bake for 10 minutes. Remove and serve.

Serves 4 to 6

LASAGNE VERDI INCASSETTATE ALLA MARCHIGIANA

Green Lasagne
Marches-Style

In this traditional lasagne from the Marches, spinach lasagne is used in a variation on Lasagne Incassettate (page 48). Some people make this dish with tagliatelle or use Gruyère cheese instead of Parmigiano-Reggiano. White truffles are very expensive—not to mention extremely hard to come by—but truffle oil, found in gourmet stores, is a good substitute.

1 recipe Green Lasagne (page 13) or 1 pound
*   commercial spinach lasagne*
1 recipe Simple Ragù alla Bolognese (page 24)
7 tablespoons unsalted butter (4 tablespoons
*   melted)*
¼ pound chicken livers, chopped
1¼ cups freshly grated Parmigiano-Reggiano
*   cheese*
1 white truffle, sliced paper-thin (optional)

1. Prepare the lasagne. Cut into 3-inch squares.

2. Prepare the Simple Ragù alla Bolognese.

3. In a small pan, melt 3 tablespoons of the butter and sauté the chicken livers over medium heat for 5 minutes, stirring occasionally. Add the chicken livers to the Ragù alla Bolognese. Check the seasoning.

4. Bring a large pot of water to a rolling boil. Salt abundantly and drop the pasta in gradually. Drain the lasagne when half-cooked and transfer to a pot of cold water until needed. Dry the lasagne before using. (Skip this step entirely if using instant lasagne.)

5. Butter a lasagne baking pan and cover the bottom with a layer of lasagne. Spoon some ragù over the lasagne and then sprinkle on some Parmigiano-Reggiano and some slices of truffle, if using. Continue layering in this order, finishing with Parmigiano-Reggiano and the melted butter.

6. Preheat the oven to 400°F. Cover the pan with a tented piece of aluminum foil and bake for 30 minutes. Serve with Parmigiano-Reggiano on the side.

Serves 6

 # LASAGNE CON VERDURE*

Lasagne with Vegetables

Here is one of my favorite lasagne. Zucchini and spinach are a perfect complement to each other in this dish of deeply satisfying flavors. It is a very light recipe and ideal served for lunch.

*1 recipe Homemade Durum-Wheat and Water
Lasagne (page 12) or 1 pound commercial
lasagne*
1 recipe Tomato Sauce (page 22)
3 tablespoons finely chopped fresh basil
1 pound fresh ricotta cheese (about 2 cups)
6 tablespoons water
Pinch of cinnamon
Salt and freshly ground black pepper
3 tablespoons olive oil
1 garlic clove, peeled and crushed
2 medium zucchini, peeled and thinly sliced
*10 ounces spinach, stems removed, washed, and
chopped*
*½ pound fresh mozzarella cheese, very thinly
sliced or shredded*
*3 tablespoons freshly grated Parmigiano-
Reggiano cheese*

1. Prepare the lasagne.
2. Prepare the tomato sauce. After you've
turned the heat off under the sauce, add the
basil and let the sauce steep.
3. If using fresh ricotta, push the ricotta
through a sieve or strainer. Stir the water, cinnamon, and salt and pepper to taste into the
ricotta until well blended.
4. Heat the olive oil in a pan and sauté the
garlic over medium-high heat until it begins to
turn light brown, about 1 minute. Leave the
garlic in the pan, add the zucchini, and sauté
for 6 minutes, stirring occasionally. Add the
spinach and salt and pepper to taste; stir and
cook 10 minutes.
5. Bring a large pot of water to a rolling boil.

Salt abundantly and drop the pasta in gradually. Drain the lasagne when half-cooked and
transfer to a pot of cold water until needed.
Dry the lasagne before using. (Skip this step
entirely if using instant lasagne.)
6. Preheat the oven to 350°F. Lightly oil the
bottom of a lasagne baking pan. Spread a tablespoon or so of tomato sauce to cover the bottom. Add layers of lasagne, ricotta, zucchini and
spinach, tomato sauce, and mozzarella, in that
order, finishing with layers of lasagne, tomato
sauce, mozzarella and Parmigiano-Reggiano.
7. Cover the lasagne with a tented piece of
aluminum foil and bake for 40 minutes.
Serves 6

▨ LASAGNE ALLA CATANESE*
Lasagne Catania-Style

This baroque recipe from Catania is typical of the
pasta dishes of eastern Sicily. The lush taste of
eggplant, sweet yellow peppers, olives, and capers
makes it as satisfying as any meat-filled lasagne.

*1 recipe Homemade Durum-Wheat and Water
Lasagne (page 12) or 1 pound commercial
lasagne*
*1 eggplant (about 1½ pounds), peeled and sliced
¼ inch thick*
¼ cup olive oil

1 small onion, peeled and very finely chopped
1 garlic clove, peeled and very finely chopped
6 tablespoons very finely chopped fresh parsley
4 salted anchovy fillets, rinsed
2 yellow bell peppers, peeled, cored, and sliced in thin strips
2 pounds ripe tomatoes, peeled, seeded, and chopped
¼ cup chopped imported green olives
¼ cup chopped imported black olives
3 tablespoons capers, rinsed (and chopped if large)
1 tablespoon dried oregano (optional)
½ cup water
Salt and freshly ground black pepper
Pure olive oil or pomace for deep-frying
1 pound thinly sliced fresh mozzarella cheese
1 cup freshly grated pecorino cheese

1. Prepare the lasagne.

2. Lay the eggplant slices on some paper towels and sprinkle with salt. Leave them to drain of their bitter juices for 1 hour, then pat dry with paper towels.

3. Meanwhile, heat the ¼ cup olive oil in a casserole. Sauté the onion, garlic, and 3 tablespoons of the parsley with the anchovies and yellow peppers over medium-high heat for 4 minutes, stirring frequently, until the anchovies have melted and the peppers are soft.

4. Reduce the heat to low and add the tomatoes, olives, capers, oregano (if using), water, and salt and pepper to taste. Simmer for 35 to 40 minutes.

5. Preheat the frying oil to 375°F. Deep-fry the eggplant slices until golden brown, about 4 to 5 minutes on a side. Drain and place on paper towels to absorb any excess oil. Reserve until needed.

6. Bring a large pot of water to a rolling boil. Salt abundantly and drop the pasta in gradually. Drain when half-cooked and transfer to a pot of cold water until needed. (Skip this step entirely if using instant lasagne.)

7. Preheat the oven to 400°F. Lightly oil a lasagne baking pan and cover the bottom with a layer of lasagne. Spoon on some sauce, add a layer of eggplant slices, mozzarella, and a sprinkling of pecorino. Continue in this order, finishing with a layer of lasagne, some sauce, and a sprinkling of pecorino. Cover the baking pan with a tented piece of aluminum foil and bake for 30 minutes. Remove, sprinkle with the remaining parsley, and either serve, cool and rebake later, or freeze.

Serves 6 to 8

PASTICCIO DI LASAGNE CON RICOTTA*

Rich Lasagne with Ricotta

This recipe was once described to me with twice the amount of butter I've called for here. After you make this delicious lasagne you will see how impossibly rich that must have been. My recipe is tailored to our less sumptuous times.

*1 recipe Homemade White Flour and Egg
    Lasagne (page 10) or 1 pound commercial
    lasagne
1 pound fresh ricotta cheese (about 2 cups)
½ cup finely chopped fresh parsley
Salt and freshly ground black pepper
¼ cup water from the lasagne pot
6 tablespoons unsalted butter, melted
1 cup freshly grated pecorino cheese*

1. Prepare the lasagne.
2. Push the ricotta through a sieve or food mill into a mixing bowl and stir in the parsley and salt and pepper to taste.
3. Bring a large pot of water to a rolling boil. Salt abundantly and drop the pasta in gradually. Drain the lasagne when al dente, saving ¼ cup cooking water, and transfer to a serving bowl. Pour the melted butter over the lasagne and toss well but gently. Stir the reserved water into the ricotta.
4. Preheat the oven to 400°F. Butter a lasagne baking pan. Interleave up to 4 layers of commercial lasagne, and more if using homemade lasagne, with the ricotta mixture. It is not necessary to unfold and perfectly arrange each sheet of lasagne. Sprinkle each layer of ricotta with pecorino. Finish layering with lasagne and some pecorino. Pour any butter remaining in the bowl that held the drained lasagne over the top and bake until the top is light golden, about 15 minutes.
    Serves 4 to 6

 # LASAGNE CON MELANZANE, NOCI, E RICOTTA*

Lasagne with Eggplant, Nuts, and Ricotta

This very rich recipe is adapted from one by the Italian gastronome Vincenzo Buonassisi. The lasagne is not layered but tossed and then baked.

*1 recipe Homemade White Flour and Egg
    Lasagne (page 10) or 1 pound commercial
    lasagne*

2 eggplants (about 2½ pounds), peeled and
sliced ¼ inch thick
3 tablespoons olive oil
2 cups tomato puree
Salt and freshly ground black pepper
Pure olive oil or pomace for deep-frying
1 cup crushed walnuts
¾ pound fresh ricotta cheese (about 1½ cups)
1½ cups freshly grated Parmigiano-Reggiano cheese

1. Prepare the lasagne. Cut into 2-inch-wide strips if using homemade.

2. Lay the eggplant slices on some paper towels and sprinkle with salt. Let them drain of their bitter juices for 1 hour or longer, then pat dry with paper towels.

3. Meanwhile, prepare a simple tomato sauce. Heat 2 tablespoons of the olive oil in a sauté pan, pour in the tomato puree, salt and pepper to taste, and cook over medium heat for 15 minutes. Cover and set aside until needed.

4. Preheat the frying oil to 375°F. Deep-fry the eggplant slices a few at a time until golden, about 4 minutes on a side. Drain on paper towels, salt, let cool, and chop.

5. In a mixing bowl, blend together two thirds each of the walnuts, eggplant, tomato sauce, and ricotta.

6. Bring a large pot of water to a rolling boil. Salt abundantly and drop the pasta in gradually. Stir a few tablespoons of the lasagne cooking water into the sauce mix. Drain the lasagne when al dente and dry. (Skip this step entirely if using instant lasagne.)

7. Preheat the oven to 400°F. Lightly oil a lasagne baking pan or pans. Toss the cooked lasagne gently with the sauce mix and arrange in the baking pan. Mix together the remaining nuts, eggplant, tomato sauce, and ricotta, and sprinkle on top. Sprinkle the Parmigiano-Reggiano over all and bake for 15 minutes.
    Serves 6

 # LASAGNE COI PISELLI E MASCARPONE*

Lasagne with Peas and Mascarpone

Although this is a vegetable lasagne, it is made with rich cheeses and is appropriate as a midwinter meal after a day of strenuous activity.

1 recipe Homemade White Flour and Egg
Lasagne (page 10) or 1 pound commercial
lasagne
1 recipe Béchamel Sauce (page 21)
2 cups fresh shelled or frozen peas
¼ pound mascarpone cheese
½ cup freshly grated Parmigiano-Reggiano
cheese
Salt and freshly ground white pepper
1 pound fresh ricotta cheese (about 2 cups)
¾ pound fresh mozzarella cheese, sliced

1. Prepare the lasagne.

2. Prepare the béchamel sauce.

3. Plunge the peas into lightly salted boiling water for 2 minutes. Drain and transfer to a mixing bowl. Stir in the mascarpone, ¼ cup of the Parmigiano-Reggiano, and salt and white pepper to taste. Set aside.

4. Bring a large pot of water to a rolling boil. Salt abundantly and drop the pasta in gradually. Drain the lasagne when half-cooked and transfer to a pot of cold water until needed. Dry the lasagne before using. (Skip this step entirely if using instant lasagne.)

5. Preheat the oven to 400°F. Butter a lasagne baking pan and layer with lasagne, one quarter of the béchamel sauce, and mozzarella. Next add layers of lasagne, ricotta, and half of the pea mixture, and then lasagne, ricotta, and mozzarella; repeat. Spoon on the remaining béchamel sauce and finally sprinkle with the remaining Parmigiano-Reggiano. Bake for 25 minutes.

Serves 6

 # LASAGNE CON BIETOLINI E MELANZANE*

Lasagne with Swiss Chard and Eggplant

This is a rich and substantial vegetable lasagne that could easily serve as a main course.

1 recipe Homemade White Flour and Egg Lasagne (page 10) or 1 pound commercial lasagne

1 medium eggplant (about 1¼ pounds), sliced ¼ inch thick

Pure olive oil or pomace for deep-frying

1¼ pounds Swiss chard, trimmed and rinsed well

3 tablespoons unsalted butter

2 tablespoons olive oil

3 garlic cloves, peeled and finely chopped

Salt and freshly ground black pepper

½ cup white wine

½ pound fresh ricotta cheese (about 1 cup)

6 tablespoons water

1 medium egg

1 cup Tomato Sauce (page 22)

¾ cup freshly grated pecorino cheese

4 ounces prosciutto (optional)

1 pound fresh mozzarella cheese, sliced

1. Prepare the lasagne.

2. Lay the eggplant slices on some paper towels and sprinkle with salt. Let them drain of their bitter juices for 1 hour or longer, then pat dry with paper towels.

3. Preheat the frying oil to 375°F. Deep-fry the eggplant slices until golden, about 3 to 4 minutes a side. Drain and reserve on a platter lined with paper towels.

4. Place the Swiss chard in a large pot with only the water from the rinsing clinging to it and turn the heat to medium-high. Cover the pot and cook until the Swiss chard wilts, about 7 minutes. Drain well and chop fine.

5. In a large sauté pan, heat the butter, olive oil, and garlic. Add the Swiss chard and salt and pepper to taste to the pan, pour in the wine, and cook over medium heat for 15 minutes, covered. Uncover and cook for 5 minutes. Let the Swiss chard cool.

6. In a mixing bowl, stir together the ricotta, water, and egg. Stir the Swiss chard into the bowl.

7. Bring a large pot of water to a rolling boil. Salt abundantly and drop the pasta in gradually. Drain the lasagne when half-cooked and transfer to a pot of cold water until needed. Dry the lasagne before using. (Skip this step entirely if using instant lasagne.)

8. Preheat the oven to 400°F. Lightly oil a lasagne baking pan. Spread a small amount of tomato sauce on the bottom and cover with a layer of lasagne. Sprinkle with pecorino, then layer on some ricotta mixture, eggplant, prosciutto (if using), mozzarella, lasagne, and

tomato sauce. Continue in this order, finishing with layers of lasagne and tomato sauce. Cover the pan with a tented piece of aluminum foil and bake for 25 minutes.

Serves 6 to 8

 # LASAGNE VERDI ALLA LIGURIA*

Green Lasagne from Liguria

Colorful markets along the Ligurian coast sell all kinds of fresh fruits and vegetables, including nettles, which some people use in making lasagne verdi instead of spinach or the beet greens I call for here.

1 recipe Green Lasagne (page 13), using beet greens (optional) instead of spinach
1 recipe Béchamel Sauce (page 21)
4 tablespoons unsalted butter

1. Prepare the lasagne.

2. Prepare the béchamel sauce.

3. Bring a large pot of water to a rolling boil. Salt abundantly and drop the pasta in gradually. Drain the lasagne when half-cooked and transfer to a pot of cold water until needed. Dry the lasagne before using. (Skip this step entirely if using instant lasagne.)

4. Butter a lasagne baking pan and layer the bottom with lasagne. Cover this layer with béchamel and continue in this order, finishing with a layer of lasagne.

5. Preheat the oven to 400°F. Dot the top of the lasagne with the remaining butter, cover with a tented piece of aluminum foil, and bake for 30 minutes.

Serves 6

 # LASAGNE VERDI CON QUATTRO FORMAGGI*

Green Lasagne with Four Cheeses

This pretty green and white lasagne dish is made with a white béchamel sauce instead of tomatoes and with four cheeses: fontina, mozzarella, pecorino, and Parmigiano-Reggiano.

1 recipe Green Lasagne (page 13) or 1 pound commercial spinach lasagne
2 recipes thick Béchamel Sauce (see page 21 and accompanying Note)
1 garlic clove, peeled and lightly crushed
¼ cup grated or finely chopped fontina cheese
¼ cup finely diced fresh mozzarella cheese
¼ cup freshly grated pecorino cheese

6 tablespoons freshly grated Parmigiano-Reggiano cheese
3 tablespoons unsalted butter

1. Prepare the lasagne.

2. Prepare the béchamel sauce and stir into it the garlic, fontina, mozzarella, pecorino, and 4 tablespoons of the Parmigiano-Reggiano. Continue stirring until the cheeses are blended. Remove and discard the garlic.

3. Bring a large pot of water to a rolling boil. Salt abundantly and drop the pasta in gradually. Drain when al dente and transfer to a pot of cold water until needed. Dry before using. (Skip this step entirely if using instant lasagne.)

4. Preheat the oven to 400°F. Butter a lasagne baking pan. Layer some lasagne on the bottom and then some sauce. Make 4 layers in all, finishing with a layer of sauce. Dot the top with the remaining butter, sprinkle with the remaining Parmigiano-Reggiano, and bake for 30 to 35 minutes.

Serves 6

PASTICCIO DI LASAGNE VERDI CON LA FONDUTA*

Rich Green Lasagne with Fondue

Fondue is popular not only in Switzerland but also in Alpine Italy. This recipe from the Piedmont uses fondue as a sauce for lasagne.

1 recipe Green Lasagne (page 13) or 1 pound commercial spinach lasagne
1 cup milk
⅓ pound fresh mozzarella cheese, diced
⅓ pound fontina cheese, diced
¼ cup heavy cream
Salt and freshly ground black pepper
3 tablespoons unsalted butter

1. Prepare the lasagne.
2. In a double boiler, heat the milk. Add the mozzarella and fontina and over medium-high heat stir until melted. Add the cream and continue stirring until the fondue is denser, about 5 minutes. Salt and pepper to taste.
3. Bring a large pot of water to a rolling boil. Salt abundantly and drop the pasta in gradually. Drain the lasagne when al dente and dry if desired. Toss the lasagne with the butter and cover the bottom of a buttered baking pan

with a layer of lasagne. Pour some sauce on top and then more lasagne, making 3 layers in all.
4. Preheat the oven to 400°F. Bake the lasagne for 20 minutes, uncovered.
Serves 4

 # LASAGNE AL FORNEL*

Oven-Baked Sweet Lasagne

From the Cordevole Valley, in the eastern Veneto, comes this lasagne, served on Christmas Eve as a first course, not a dessert.

1 recipe Homemade White Flour and Egg Lasagne (page 10) or 1 pound commercial lasagne
4 cups grated Granny Smith apples (about 4 apples)
1 cup golden raisins, soaked in tepid water for 30 minutes
½ cup dried figs, finely chopped
1 cup coarsely ground walnuts
1 tablespoon poppy seeds
⅓ cup sugar
10 tablespoons unsalted butter, melted
¼ cup water

1. Prepare the lasagne.
2. Mix together the apples, raisins, figs, walnuts, and poppy seeds.

3. Bring a large pot of water to a rolling boil. Salt abundantly and drop the pasta in gradually. Drain the lasagne when half-cooked and transfer to a pot of cold water until needed. Dry the lasagne before using. (Skip this step entirely if using instant lasagne.)

4. Preheat the oven to 350°F. Butter a lasagne baking pan and cover the bottom with a layer of lasagne. Sprinkle with some of the apple-and-poppy-seed mixture and then some sugar (reserve 2 teaspoons) and drizzle with some melted butter (reserve 2 tablespoons). Continue in this order, finishing with a layer of lasagne. Sprinkle with the remaining sugar, drizzle with the remaining butter, and pour the water over the top. Cover with a tented piece of aluminum foil and bake for 45 to 50 minutes.

Serves 4 to 6

4

FREE-FORM LASAGNE

 ## LASAGNE AL SUGO

Lasagne with Meat Sauce

This is a traditional tossed lasagne preparation from Genoa. By *lasagne* Genoese mean dough cut into 2½-inch squares. The beef broth is thickened with browned flour in this recipe, a method not often found in Italy. In the final assembly the lasagne is layered with sauce and Parmigiano-Reggiano cheese and served immediately.

*1 recipe Homemade White Flour and Egg
   Lasagne (page 10) or 1 pound commercial
   lasagne*
4 tablespoons unsalted butter
1 onion, peeled and finely chopped
1 carrot, peeled and finely chopped
1 celery stalk, finely chopped
¼ cup finely chopped fresh parsley
½ pound veal shoulder, diced
½ pound beef sirloin, diced
⅓ cup white wine
*2 pounds ripe tomatoes, peeled, seeded, and
   chopped*
Salt and freshly ground black pepper
*1 tablespoon all-purpose bleached or unbleached
   flour*
¾ cup hot Beef Broth (page 28)
½ cup freshly grated Parmigiano-Reggiano cheese

1. Prepare the lasagne. Cut into 2½-inch squares.

2. In a casserole, melt the butter and sauté the onion, carrot, celery, parsley, veal, and beef over medium heat until the onion is soft, about 12 minutes. Pour in the wine, turn the heat up to high, and cook uncovered until the wine has evaporated, about 4 minutes. Add the tomatoes and salt and pepper to taste. Cover, reduce the heat to low, and simmer for 35 minutes.

3. In a small pan, cook the flour over medium-high heat, until it turns golden brown, about 5 to 6 minutes. Slowly pour in the hot beef broth, stirring constantly and vigorously. Add this mixture to the tomato-meat sauce, stirring well to blend. Cover and simmer until the meat is tender, about 1 hour.

4. Bring a large pot of water to a rolling boil. Salt abundantly and drop the pasta in gradually. Drain the lasagne when al dente and layer some of it on the bottom of a serving bowl or platter. Ladle on some sauce, sprinkle on some Parmigiano-Reggiano, and continue in this order until all the lasagne and sauce are used up. Serve immediately.

Serves 4 to 6

 # LASAGNE DI GIOVEDÌ GRASSO
Lasagne for Fat Thursday

In Naples this traditional preparation for Fat Thursday — the week before the end of Carnival marking the end of the pre-Lenten season — is eaten as a first course, followed by the braised pork and sausages used to make Sugo di Umido di Maiale and seasonal vegetables flavored with olive oil and garlic.

> *1 recipe Homemade Durum-Wheat and Water Lasagne (page 12) or 1 pound commercial lasagne*
> *2½ cups Sugo di Umido di Maiale (page 25)*
> *½ cup water from the lasagne pot*
> *1 pound fresh ricotta cheese (about 2 cups)*
> *1 cup freshly grated Parmigiano-Reggiano cheese*

1. Prepare the lasagne.

2. Prepare the Sugo di Umido di Maiale.

3. Bring a large pot of water to a rolling boil. Salt abundantly and drop the pasta in gradually.

4. While the lasagne is cooking, remove ½ cup water from the pot and stir into the ricotta, mixing until it is thick and creamy.

5. Drain the lasagne when al dente and transfer to a serving platter. Layer the lasagne with ricotta, three quarters of the pork sauce, and three quarters of the Parmigiano-Reggiano. Serve

with the remaining Parmigiano-Reggiano and pork sauce on the side.

Serves 6 (8 with the meat)

 ## "PICCAGGE" AL SUGO

Ligurian-Style Lasagne with Veal Sauce

Piccagge is Genovese dialect for pappardelle, a broad egg pasta that belongs to the lasagne category. *Piccagge in bianco,* a well-known regional dish, is seasoned only with butter and Parmigiano-Reggiano. It is made with white flour, egg, and water and is cut into ribbons from ½ inch to 4 inches wide. This recipe takes the basic *piccagge* or lasagne and coats it with a rich meat sauce. Some people serve the meat separately as a second course, with a salad.

   1 recipe Homemade White Flour and Egg Lasagne (page 10), cut in 4-inch-wide strips, or ¾ pound commercial lasagne
½ cup dried mushrooms
4 tablespoons unsalted butter
¾ pound lean veal (either tenderloin, cut into scallopine, or shoulder, cut in small pieces)
1 medium onion, peeled and finely chopped
1½ pounds ripe tomatoes, peeled, seeded, and finely chopped

Salt and freshly ground black pepper
1 tablespoon all-purpose bleached or unbleached flour
½ cup freshly grated Parmigiano-Reggiano cheese

1. Prepare the lasagne.
2. Soak the dried mushrooms for 30 minutes in tepid water. Drain and chop.
3. In a sauté pan, melt the butter and brown the veal with the onion over medium-high heat for 6 minutes, stirring constantly. Add the tomatoes, mushrooms, and salt and pepper to taste. Cover, reduce the heat to medium, and cook for 12 minutes. Turn the heat off and let rest until needed.
4. Meanwhile, heat the flour in a small sauté pan until it turns a light brown, about 2 minutes. Transfer the flour to the sauce. Add a small amount of water if the sauce looks too dry.
5. Bring a large pot of water to a rolling boil. Salt abundantly and drop the pasta in gradually. Drain when al dente and transfer to a serving platter or bowl. Cover with the sauce and Parmigiano-Reggiano. Toss well before serving.

Serves 4 to 6

LASAGNE AI FUNGHI
Lasagne with Mushrooms

Calabrians, from Italy's south, love mushrooms, as in this lasagne with its thick tomato sauce, but they also like spicy-hot foods. In this recipe I use two hot fresh chili peppers, one green and one red. The sauce can also be served with lasagnette.

> *1 recipe Homemade Durum-Wheat and Water Lasagne (page 12) or 1 pound commercial lasagne*
> *½ pound lean ground beef*
> *1 small onion, peeled*
> *½ cup fresh parsley leaves*
> *4 tablespoons commercial pork lard*
> *1 pound mushrooms, cleaned and sliced*
> *2 cups tomato puree*
> *2 fresh chili peppers (1 green, 1 red), seeded and chopped, or ¾ teaspoon red chili pepper flakes*
> *Salt*

1. Prepare the lasagne.
2. In a casserole, brown the ground beef over medium heat until it loses its pinkness. Remove the meat with a slotted spoon, draining off and discarding any fat, and set aside. Finely chop the onion and parsley together.
3. Melt the lard in the same casserole over medium heat and sauté the onion and parsley for 4 minutes, stirring. Add the mushrooms and continue cooking for 5 minutes, stirring frequently. Pour the tomato puree into the casserole and mix with the mushrooms. Add the chili peppers or red chili pepper flakes, cooked ground beef, and salt to taste. Stir well, cover, and cook for 30 minutes. Moisten the sauce with up to ½ cup water.
4. Meanwhile, bring a large pot of water to a rolling boil. Salt abundantly and drop the pasta in gradually. Drain the lasagne when al dente and transfer to the casserole, tossing gently and thoroughly with the mushroom sauce before serving.

Serves 4 to 6

 # LASAGNE COI FAGIOLI
Lasagne with White Beans

This is a typical home preparation from Basilicata, the instep of the Italian boot. The pasta is made with durum wheat and water only. In Lucania, another name for Basilicata, people do not eat this dish with grated cheese.

> *½ pound dried small white beans*
> *1 recipe Homemade Durum-Wheat and Water Lasagne (page 12) or 1 pound commercial lasagne*
> *2 ounces finely diced salt pork*
> *2 garlic cloves, peeled and lightly crushed*

2 tablespoons olive oil
Salt and freshly ground black pepper
¼ cup finely chopped fresh parsley

1. Soak the beans overnight in cold water.
2. Prepare the lasagne.
3. Bring a pot of lightly salted water to a boil and cook the beans until tender, about 1¼ hours. Drain and reserve.
4. In a large pan, sauté the salt pork and garlic in the olive oil over medium heat until the garlic begins to turn light brown. Remove and discard the garlic. Add the beans to the pan, salt lightly, and stir. Reduce the heat to very low while you cook the pasta.
5. Bring a large pot of water to a rolling boil. Salt abundantly and drop the pasta in gradually. Drain the lasagne when al dente. Transfer to a serving bowl or platter. Mix well with the beans and salt pork. Sprinkle with abundant black pepper and the parsley, and serve.
Serves 4

 # LASAGNE CON CIPOLLE
Lasagne with Onions

This is a simple recipe and a specialty of the villages of the Apennines near Bologna, in Emilia-Romagna.

1 recipe Homemade White Flour and Egg
*   Lasagne (page 10) or 1 pound commercial*
*   lasagne*
3 tablespoons olive oil
8 ounces finely diced pancetta
1½ pounds peeled and thinly sliced white onions
¾ cup water
Salt and freshly ground black pepper
Freshly grated Parmigiano-Reggiano cheese
*   (optional)*

1. Prepare the lasagne.
2. Heat the olive oil in a large sauté pan over medium heat and brown the pancetta for 10 minutes, stirring occasionally. Add the onions, water, and salt and pepper to taste, and continue cooking, stirring often, for 15 minutes.
3. Bring a large pot of water to a rolling boil. Salt abundantly and drop the pasta in gradually. Drain the lasagne when al dente and transfer to a serving platter or bowl. Toss with the onion sauce and serve immediately with Parmigiano-Reggiano, if desired.
Serves 4 to 6

"STRASCINATA" CON "LA SBREFFATA"

This rustic preparation is typical of Apulia, Calabria, and Basilicata. *Strascinata* is a kind of lasagne that has had the tines of a fork drawn across it. In the south an instrument called a *cavarola,* a ridged wooden board, is used. *Strascinata* means drawn or pulled across in Apulian dialect, and *sbreffata* is Apulian for how the almonds are prepared: they are roasted and then ground in the mouth before being sprinkled on the pasta or soup. You will find your food processor useful in place of authenticity.

This recipe, from the villages near Brindisi, is adapted from one by Italian author Luigi Sada. The peasants consider it a *minestra,* or soup, when they eat it during the days of Lent.

1 recipe Homemade Durum-Wheat and Water Lasagne (see page 12 and step 1 below) or
1 pound commercial lasagne
⅔ cup olive oil
⅓ cup fresh bread crumbs
4 salted anchovy fillets, rinsed
Freshly ground black pepper
⅓ cup ground almonds

1. Prepare the lasagne or *strascinata*. Roll out to a thickness of ¹⁄₃₂ inch or 1 millimeter. After the final rolling, draw the tines of a fork lengthwise across the lasagne. Dry for 2 hours.

2. Heat the olive oil in a frying pan over high heat until it is almost smoking. Reduce the heat to medium and after 2 minutes sauté the bread crumbs, anchovies, and abundant black pepper for 2 minutes, stirring frequently. Turn the heat off, stir in the almonds, and set aside until needed, stirring occasionally.

3. Bring a large pot of water to a rolling boil. Salt abundantly and drop the pasta in gradually. Drain the lasagne when al dente and transfer to a serving platter or bowl. Toss well with the sauce, making sure each sheet of lasagne is coated.
Serves 4 to 6

 # LASAGNE CACATE DI MODICA
Shitty Lasagne from Modica

Sicilians love vulgar names for their favorite dishes. The name of this rough-and-ready peasant preparation is mild compared with some others I've come across, but it in no way looks bad. When I make this lusty lasagne my guests can't stop eating it. The recipe is very authentic, since in Sicily, especially in the smaller villages of the interior, cooks still make *pasta casarecchia,* homemade pasta. Traditionally this lasagne is served as a *piatto unico,* a single-course dinner, on New Year's Eve. Try sprinkling on ricotta salata, a hard, dried ricotta used for grating, instead of pecorino.

3 cups all-purpose bleached or unbleached flour
3 large eggs
1 teaspoon salt
½ pound ground beef
½ pound sweet Italian sausage
¼ cup olive oil
¼ cup peeled and very finely chopped onions
1 garlic clove, peeled and very finely chopped
1 cup tomato puree
2 tablespoons tomato paste
½ cup hot water
Salt and freshly ground black pepper
½ pound fresh ricotta cheese (about 1 cup), crumbled
¼ to ½ cup freshly grated pecorino cheese or grated ricotta salata

1. Pour the flour onto a work surface. Make a well in the middle and break the eggs into it. Sprinkle in the salt. Begin to incorporate the eggs with the flour, a little at a time, with your fingers, pulling more flour from the inside wall of the well. Once the flour and eggs are combined, knead for about 8 minutes until you can form a smooth ball, using a few tablespoons of water if necessary. Wrap the dough in wax paper, plastic wrap, or aluminum foil, and let rest for 30 minutes at room temperature.

2. With a rolling pin, roll the pasta out until it can fit into the roller of a pasta-rolling machine. Roll out into very thin sheets and with a knife cut them into 1-inch-wide strips. Lay on a white sheet draped over a table to dry for several hours.

3. In a sauté pan, cook the beef and sausage together over medium-high heat until there is no pink remaining. Drain the meat with a slotted spoon, discarding the fat. Set the meat aside.

4. In the same pan, heat the olive oil over medium heat and sauté the onions and garlic until the onions are translucent, about 3 minutes, stirring frequently so the garlic doesn't burn. Add the cooked meat, reduce the heat to low, and stir. Add the tomato puree, tomato paste, hot water, and salt and pepper to taste, and cook for 30 minutes.

5. Bring a large pot of water to a rolling boil. Salt abundantly and drop the pasta in gradually. Drain when al dente and transfer to a large serving platter. Cover with the meat sauce and sprinkle on the fresh ricotta. Toss well and sprinkle on the pecorino or ricotta salata.

Serves 4 to 6

"SCIABBÒ"

This Sicilian specialty from the inland town of Enna uses a fresh homemade *lasagne ricce*, ruffle-edged lasagne. *Sciabbò* and *scibbò* are old Sicilian words for the ruffles on the edges of the lasagne sheet and derive from the French *jabot*, indicating the frills on the front of a dress shirt. The unusual addition of chocolate is a legacy of Spanish rule in Sicily.

*1 recipe Homemade White Flour and Egg
    Lasagne (page 10) or 1 pound commercial
    lasagne ricce*
½ cup olive oil
1 medium onion, peeled and thinly sliced
*½ pound chopped pork, cut from the neck or
    shoulder*
½ cup red wine
1½ cups tomato puree
Salt and freshly ground black pepper
1 tablespoon sugar
Pinch of cinnamon
1 ounce melted sweet chocolate

1. Prepare the lasagne. Cut into strips 3 inches wide.

2. Heat the olive oil in a sauté pan and sauté the onion over medium heat until translucent, about 8 minutes. Add the pork and brown, about 5 minutes. Pour in the wine and then the tomato puree; add salt and pepper to taste. Cover, reduce the heat to medium-low, and cook for 30 minutes, moistening the sauce with water if it appears to be drying out. After the sauce has cooked for 30 minutes, stir in the sugar, cinnamon, and chocolate, and continue cooking for 10 minutes.

3. Meanwhile, bring a large pot of water to a rolling boil. Salt abundantly and drop the pasta in gradually. Drain when al dente and transfer the lasagne to a serving platter or bowl and cover with the sauce, tossing gently.

Serves 4 to 6

 # LASAGNE COL RAGÙ

Lasagne with Meat Sauce

This recipe from Abruzzi is often made with *maccheroni alla chitarra*, a kind of spaghetti pressed through a device strung with guitar wire (hence the name), but here lasagne is used. The chili pepper flakes make the flavorful sauce hot, the way the Abruzzese like it.

*1 recipe Homemade Durum-Wheat and Water
    Lasagne (page 12) or 1 pound commercial
    lasagne*
*4 tablespoons 'nzugna (freshly rendered pork
    fat) (see page 25), commercial pork lard, or
    vegetable shortening*
1 small onion, peeled and finely chopped
1 carrot, peeled and finely chopped
½ celery stalk, finely chopped
2 garlic cloves, peeled and finely chopped

2 tablespoons finely chopped fresh parsley
1 tablespoon unsalted butter
2 pounds pork shoulder or chop, in 1 piece
Salt
1 teaspoon red chili pepper flakes
1 cup dry white wine
3 pounds ripe tomatoes, peeled, seeded, and
    chopped
¼ cup water from the lasagne pot
½ pound fresh ricotta cheese (about 1 cup)
½ cup freshly grated pecorino cheese

1. Prepare the lasagne.

2. Melt the *'nzugna,* lard, or shortening in a casserole and sauté the onion, carrot, celery, garlic, and parsley over medium-high heat for 4 to 5 minutes, stirring frequently. Add the butter and when it melts, add the pork. Mix well, salt to taste, and sprinkle with ½ teaspoon of the red chili pepper flakes. Brown the meat on all sides over medium-high heat for 5 minutes.

3. Pour in the wine and cook until it is evaporated. Add the tomatoes, mix well, and bring to a boil. Reduce to low and cook for 3 to 4 hours, uncovered.

4. Remove the meat and serve as a second course with some of the sauce, if desired. Strain the sauce through a strainer. Push the remaining sauce through a food mill and set it aside to cool. Place in the refrigerator until the fat congeals. Once the layer of fat has formed on top, remove and discard it.

5. Bring a large pot of water to a rolling boil. Salt abundantly and drop the pasta in gradually. Drain the lasagne when al dente, saving ¼ cup cooking water, and dry if desired.

6. Stir the reserved cooking water into the ricotta until it is smooth and creamy. Transfer the lasagne to a serving platter or bowl, cover with 3 cups of the sauce (save the remainder for another use), and toss. Sprinkle with the ricotta and the remaining red pepper flakes and toss again. Toss a final time with the pecorino and serve.

Variation: Add ½ pound cooked sausage, sliced or crumbled, and 3 tablespoons unsalted melted butter to the lasagne.

Serves 4 to 6

LASAGNE RICCE CON POLLO
Ruffle-Edged Lasagne with Chicken

Lasagne ricce simply refers to the ruffled edges of the lasagne. This is a free-form dish typical of northern Italian family cooking. If you are unable to find caciocavallo, replace it with imported provolone.

1 recipe Homemade White Flour and Egg
    Lasagne (page 10) or ½ pound commercial
    lasagne ricce
¾ pound chicken breast, cut up into bite-size
    pieces

Flour for dredging
4 tablespoons unsalted butter
2 tablespoons olive oil
4 ounces pancetta, finely diced
1 onion, peeled and thinly sliced
¼ pound fresh porcini or portobello mushrooms, cleaned and thinly sliced
2 green bell peppers, peeled, cored, and thinly sliced
2 tablespoons water
1 cup finely chopped ripe tomatoes
6 tablespoons Marsala wine
Salt and freshly ground black pepper
½ cup freshly grated caciocavallo cheese

1. Prepare the lasagne.
2. Dredge the chicken in the flour and shake off any excess. Melt 3 tablespoons of the butter in a saucepan over medium-high heat and when it stops bubbling, add the chicken and sauté until golden, about 4 minutes. Remove and reserve.
3. In a skillet, heat the olive oil and sauté the pancetta over medium heat for 8 minutes, stirring occasionally. Add the onion, mushrooms, bell peppers, and water, and simmer over medium heat for 15 minutes.
4. Add the tomatoes and Marsala to the skillet, cover, and cook for 20 minutes. Add the reserved chicken, salt and pepper to taste, and continue cooking for 2 minutes. Turn the heat off, add the remaining 1 tablespoon butter, and keep covered and warm while you cook the pasta.
5. Bring a large pot of water to a rolling boil.

Salt abundantly and drop the pasta in gradually. Drain the lasagne when al dente and toss with the sauce. Serve immediately with the caciocavallo.

Serves 4

 # LASAGNE ALLA FINANZIERA
Fancy Lasagne in the Financier's Style

This preparation is typical in Lombardy and Liguria. It is sometimes made with coxcomb, *cresta di gallo,* and called *lasagne alla Cavour* for Count Cavour, who was instrumental in Italy's struggle for unification.

1 recipe Homemade White Flour and Egg Lasagne (page 10) or 1 pound commercial lasagne
3 tablespoons unsalted butter
2 tablespoons olive oil
2 ounces pancetta, very finely chopped
1 medium onion, peeled and very finely chopped
1 bouquet garni (6 fresh basil leaves, 6 fresh sage leaves, and 1 bay leaf tied together in cheesecloth)
¾ pound chicken livers, finely chopped
¼ pound chicken hearts, finely chopped

¼ cup brandy
1 cup Chicken Broth (page 28)
Salt and freshly ground black pepper
1 cup freshly grated Parmigiano-Reggiano cheese

1. Prepare the lasagne.

2. Place the butter and olive oil in a casserole and turn the heat to medium. When the butter has melted, add the pancetta, onion, and bouquet garni, and sauté for 8 minutes, stirring frequently. Add the chicken livers and hearts and continue cooking for 10 minutes, stirring. Pour in the brandy, chicken broth, and salt and pepper to taste. Cook until the liquid is reduced by half, about 8 to 10 minutes. Remove and discard the bouquet garni. Check the seasoning and correct.

3. Bring a large pot of water to a rolling boil. Salt abundantly and drop the pasta in gradually. Drain the lasagne when al dente. Pour a few tablespoons of sauce into a serving platter or bowl. Transfer some lasagne to the bowl and pour more sauce on top. Continue in this manner until all the sauce and lasagne are used up, sprinkling Parmigiano-Reggiano over each layer and on top. Serve with more Parmigiano-Reggiano, if desired.

Serves 4 to 6

 # LASAGNE RICCE CON L'ANITRA

Ruffle-Edged Lasagne with Duck

This recipe is from the Varese and Brianza regions of Lombardy, where lakes support a population of waterfowl, including duck. Traditionally the hunter-farmer shoots the birds and brings them home for his wife to prepare. Remember that ducks have a lot of fat, which must be removed.

1 recipe Homemade White Flour and Egg Lasagne (page 10) or 1 pound commercial lasagne ricce
1 duck (about 4½ to 5 pounds)
4 tablespoons unsalted butter
1 tablespoon olive oil
1 medium onion, peeled and finely chopped
2 pounds ripe tomatoes, peeled, seeded, and chopped
1 cup red wine
½ teaspoon dried rosemary
½ teaspoon dried oregano
Salt and freshly ground black pepper
1 duck liver

1. Prepare the lasagne. Cut into strips 1½ inches wide and 9 to 12 inches long.

2. Carve the duck into 2 breasts and 2 legs with thighs. Save the liver and chop fine; set aside. Remove and discard all skin and fat. Save the wings, neck, heart, gizzard, and carcass to make a duck stock some other time.

3. Place the butter with the olive oil in a casserole over medium-high heat. When the butter stops bubbling, brown the duck pieces for 2 to 3 minutes a side. Remove and set aside.

4. Reduce the heat to medium and sauté the onion for 4 to 5 minutes, stirring frequently and scraping the bottom of the casserole. Add the tomatoes, reduce the heat to low, and simmer for 25 minutes.

5. Pour the wine into the casserole and stir. Sprinkle in the rosemary, oregano, and salt and pepper to taste, and stir. Return the duck to the casserole and simmer uncovered for 1 hour or until it is tender, turning the pieces now and then and stirring occasionally.

6. Remove the duck pieces and slice thin. Cut, scrape, or pull off any remaining fat and discard. Slice the meat off the leg bones and discard the bones. Add the duck liver to the casserole and cook for 5 minutes. Return the duck meat to the casserole, stir, turn off the heat, and cover until the pasta is ready.

7. Bring a large pot of water to a rolling boil. Salt abundantly and drop the pasta in gradually. Drain the lasagne when al dente, transfer to a serving platter or bowl, and pour the sauce over. Serve immediately.

Serves 4 to 6

 # LASAGNE CON LA LEPRE IN SALAMOIA
Lasagne with Wine-Marinated Rabbit

Marinated rabbit replaces the traditional hare in this recipe. The lasagne is tossed with the sauce and the rabbit laid on top with Parmigiano-Reggiano sprinkled about. I couldn't quite believe it, but my children love this dish.

> *1 recipe Homemade White Flour and Egg Lasagne (page 10) or 1 pound commercial lasagne*
> *1 rabbit (about 4 pounds), cut into 8 pieces*
> *1 quart water*
> *1 quart red wine vinegar*
> *15 black peppercorns*
> *5 garlic cloves, peeled, 3 crushed*
> *3 bay leaves*
> *2 fresh rosemary sprigs*
> *⅓ cup olive oil*
> *Salt and freshly ground black pepper*
> *½ cup red wine*
> *¼ cup Tomato Sauce (page 22)*
> *¼ cup water*
> *¾ cup freshly grated Parmigiano-Reggiano cheese*

1. Prepare the lasagne.

2. Place the rabbit in a deep, preferably earthenware or ceramic pot or bowl with the water and vinegar to cover by an inch. Add the peppercorns, crushed garlic, bay leaves, and 1 of the rosemary sprigs. Cover and refrigerate for 24 hours.

3. Remove the rabbit pieces, drain, and damp-dry well with paper towels. Finely chop the remaining 2 garlic cloves and the leaves from the other rosemary sprig together. Heat the olive oil in a casserole and sauté the garlic-and-rosemary mixture over medium heat for 30 seconds. Add the rabbit pieces and salt and pepper to taste. Cook for 10 minutes, turning several times. Pour in the wine and when it has evaporated, in 12 to 15 minutes, add the tomato sauce and water. Cover and cook for 30 minutes. Uncover and cook for another 15 minutes.

4. Bring a large pot of water to a rolling boil. Salt abundantly and drop the pasta in gradually. Drain the lasagne when al dente and transfer to a deep serving bowl or platter. Ladle enough sauce over the lasagne so that all the sheets are coated. Sprinkle with ½ cup of the Parmigiano-Reggiano and toss. Place the pieces of rabbit on top, sprinkle the remaining Parmigiano-Reggiano over the rabbit, and serve.

Serves 4

 # LASAGNE MARINARA
Lasagne with Seafood

This tossed lasagne from Campania is made with shellfish and a rich tomato sauce.

1 recipe Homemade White Flour and Egg
   Lasagne (page 10) or 1 pound commercial
   lasagne
¼ cup olive oil
1 onion, peeled and chopped
4 garlic cloves, peeled and chopped
½ cup finely chopped fresh parsley
1 six-ounce can tomato paste
2 cups white wine, or more if necessary
2 cups crushed tomatoes
Salt and freshly ground black pepper
12 oysters, scrubbed well
24 littleneck clams, scrubbed well
36 mussels, debearded and scrubbed well

1. Prepare the lasagne.

2. In a large pot that will hold all the shellfish, heat the olive oil over medium-high heat and sauté the onion, garlic, and parsley for 3 to 4 minutes, stirring constantly so the garlic doesn't burn. Dissolve the tomato paste in the 2 cups wine and pour into the pot along with the tomatoes; add salt and pepper to taste. Reduce the heat to low and simmer for 45 minutes, moistening with more wine if necessary.

3. Raise the heat to medium-high and add the oysters. After 8 minutes add the clams. After another 8 minutes add the mussels and continue cooking until the mussels open, about 15 to 20 minutes. Take the oysters, clams, and mussels out of the pot; remove the meats from the shells and set aside.

4. Bring a large pot of water to a rolling boil. Salt abundantly and drop the pasta in gradually. Drain when al dente and toss with the tomato sauce and the reserved oysters, clams, and mussels. Serve immediately.

Serves 4

 # LASAGNE NERE CON SUGO DI SEPPIA
Black Lasagne with Cuttlefish Sauce

This unusual free-form lasagne from Venice is startling in appearance and very flavorful. For a dramatic presentation at the table I recommend white bowls. If you opt to use regular lasagne instead of making your own black lasagne, replace the cuttlefish with squid.

1 recipe Black Lasagne (page 13)
¼ cup olive oil
1 small onion, peeled and finely chopped
1 garlic clove, peeled and crushed

3 tablespoons finely chopped fresh parsley
⅓ cup white wine
1½ pounds ripe tomatoes, peeled, seeded, and chopped
Salt and freshly ground black pepper
¾ pound (about 1 cup) cuttlefish or squid (if not making black lasagne), cleaned and chopped
¼ cup water

1. Prepare the lasagne.

2. In a sauté pan, heat the olive oil and sauté the onion, garlic, and 2 tablespoons of the parsley over medium heat for 5 minutes, stirring frequently. Pour in the wine and tomatoes, and add salt and pepper to taste; cook for 15 minutes. Add the cuttlefish or squid and water, reduce the heat to low, and simmer for 45 minutes.

3. Bring a large pot of water to a rolling boil. Salt abundantly and drop the pasta in gradually. Drain the lasagne when al dente and dry. Transfer to a serving platter or bowl and pour the sauce on top with a sprinkling of the remaining parsley. Serve immediately.

Serves 4 to 6

"LAGANE" E COZZE

Lasagne and Mussels

This family-style lasagne is common in the area around Bari, in Apulia. It is made with a pasta called *lanache* or *lagane*, dialect for homemade, hand-cut lasagne about an inch wide. In Apulian homes it is known simply as *lagane di casa*, homemade wide tagliatelle.

> 1 recipe Homemade Durum-Wheat and Water
>   Lasagne (page 12) or 1 pound commercial
>   lasagne
> 1 small onion, peeled and finely chopped
> 2 garlic cloves, peeled and finely chopped
> 4 large fresh basil leaves, finely chopped
> ¼ cup olive oil
> 1 pound ripe plum tomatoes, peeled, seeded, and
>   chopped
> Salt
> ½ cup finely chopped fresh parsley
> 2 cups fresh bread crumbs
> 1 cup freshly grated pecorino cheese
> 3 egg yolks
> Freshly ground black pepper
> 1½ to 2 pounds large mussels, debearded and
>   scrubbed well
> Freshly grated pecorino cheese (optional)

1. Prepare the lasagne. Cut into 1-inch strips.
2. In a large pan or casserole, sauté the onion, 1 of the garlic cloves, and basil in the olive oil over medium-high heat, stirring frequently, until the onion is soft and translucent, about 4 to 5 minutes. Add the tomatoes, salt to taste, and reduce the heat to medium-low. Cook the sauce for 20 minutes.
3. In a bowl, mix together the parsley, the remaining garlic, and the bread crumbs, pecorino, egg yolks, and black pepper to taste. Blend this stuffing mixture well. If it is too soft, add more bread crumbs or cheese.
4. Open the mussels slightly over a bowl. Open only enough to stuff them, reserving any liquid. This sounds hard, but it isn't, since the mussels will already be slightly open. Use your fingers, a teaspoon, or a small butter knife to open the mussels and push about 1 teaspoon stuffing into each mussel, being careful not to open them so much as to detach them from their shell. Strain the liquid and reserve, if any. Squeeze the mussels closed again, as much as you can, and arrange in the tomato sauce. Cover the pan or casserole, raise the heat to medium, and cook for 15 minutes, until the mussels are cooked, shaking the pan or casserole occasionally.
5. Bring a large pot of water to a rolling boil. Salt abundantly and drop the pasta in gradually. Drain well when al dente and transfer to a serving bowl or platter. Pour the sauce and mussels over the lasagne and toss slightly and gently. Serve with a light sprinkling of grated pecorino, if desired.

Serves 4 to 6

LASAGNE AL SUGO D'ANGUILLA
Lasagne with Eel Sauce

In Apulia, the heel of the Italian boot, lasagne is called *lagane* or *laane* and is cut into the size of a wide Christmas ribbon. The sauce in this recipe is made of common eel (*Anguilla anguilla* L.), a rich fish with a taste very close to that of shark and easily replaced with ocean pout, both of which work here because they taste good and are easier to find than fresh eel. You could also make this lasagne with mackerel fillets, in which case the fillets should be left whole.

> *1 recipe Durum-Wheat and Water Lasagne*
> *(page 12) or 1 pound commercial lasagne*
> *1¼ cups olive oil*
> *1 pound eel, shark, dogfish, or ocean pout, cut*
> *into ¾-inch cubes, without bone*
> *Flour for dredging*
> *3 garlic cloves, peeled and finely chopped*
> *¼ cup finely chopped fresh parsley*
> *¼ cup finely chopped fresh basil*
> *2 cups tomato puree*
> *Salt and freshly ground black pepper*

1. Prepare the lasagne. Cut into 1½-inch-wide strips.

2. Heat 1 cup of the oil in a pan over high heat. Dredge the fish in the flour, shaking off any excess. When the oil is nearly smoking, fry the fish until golden, about 90 seconds. Remove from the oil with a slotted spoon or tongs and drain on paper towels.

3. In a casserole, heat the remaining 4 tablespoons olive oil over medium heat and sauté the garlic, parsley, and basil for 1 minute. Add the tomato puree, and salt and pepper to taste. Cover, reduce the heat to low, and cook for 15 minutes. Add a few tablespoons of water if necessary to keep the sauce moist.

4. Add the fish to the tomato sauce, raise the heat to medium, and cook 6 minutes.

5. Bring a large pot of water to a rolling boil. Salt abundantly and drop the pasta in gradually. Drain the lasagne when al dente and transfer to the sauce casserole, tossing gently. Serve immediately.

Serves 4 to 6

 # LASAGNE "D'ARBITRIU"*
Free-Style Lasagne

In households of the hamlets dotting mountainous Sicily, ruffle-edged lasagne, *lasagne ricce,* is made with an apparatus called an *arbitriu.* Pino Correnti, the Sicilian food authority, reports that older versions of this dish call for chocolate, *vino cotto* (a cooked wine), cinnamon, and other spices. This recipe is the very simplest one, but I recommend, because of this, that you use homemade lasagne and homemade tomato sauce.

> 1 recipe Homemade Durum-Wheat and Water
> Lasagne (page 12) or 1 pound commercial
> lasagne
> 1 recipe Tomato Sauce (page 22)
> ½ teaspoon ground cinnamon (optional)
> Freshly grated Parmigiano-Reggiano cheese
> (optional)

1. Prepare the lasagne.

2. Prepare the tomato sauce and add the cinnamon if using.

3. Bring a large pot of water to a rolling boil. Salt abundantly and drop the pasta in gradually. Drain the lasagne when al dente and transfer to a serving bowl. Toss with the tomato sauce and serve with Parmigiano-Reggiano cheese, if desired.

Serves 4

 LASAGNE ALLA MOZZARELLA*

Lasagne with Mozzarella

This all-white free-form lasagne is made with fresh mozzarella and freshly grated Parmigiano-Reggiano cheese. It can be made spicier by a liberal hand with the black pepper.

> 1 recipe Homemade White Flour and Egg
> Lasagne (page 10) or 1 pound commercial
> lasagne
> 8 tablespoons unsalted butter
> 8 salted anchovy fillets, rinsed
> ½ pound fresh mozzarella cheese, diced tiny
> Freshly ground black pepper
> ½ cup freshly grated Parmigiano-Reggiano cheese

1. Prepare the lasagne.

2. Bring a large pot of water to a rolling boil. Salt abundantly and drop the pasta in gradually. Drain the lasagne when al dente and dry.

3. Meanwhile, melt the butter in a casserole over medium heat and add the anchovies. Mash the anchovies with the back of a wooden spoon and once they have melted, reduce the heat to very low.

4. Add the lasagne to the casserole, tossing gently but well. Add the mozzarella, making sure it doesn't clump, and continue tossing. When the mozzarella begins to string, pepper it to taste and sprinkle with the Parmigiano-Reggiano. Continue tossing gently. Transfer to a serving platter, sprinkle with a bit more coarsely ground black pepper, and serve.

Serves 4 to 6

LASAGNETTE AL MASCARPONE*

Lasagnette with Mascarpone Cheese

This delightfully simple preparation is made with a very narrow lasagne called by the diminutive *lasagnette*. But the taste is not at all diminutive — it is creamy, cheesy, and delicious.

1 recipe Homemade White Flour and Egg Lasagne (page 10) or ¾ pound commercial lasagnette
2 egg yolks
3 tablespoons olive oil
½ cup mascarpone cheese
Salt and freshly ground black pepper
½ cup freshly grated Parmigiano-Reggiano cheese

1. Prepare the lasagne. Cut into ¾-inch-wide strips.
2. In a mixing bowl, place the egg yolks and slowly beat in the olive oil, in a very thin stream, beating all the time, as you would if making a mayonnaise. Add the mascarpone a little at a time and add salt and pepper to taste.
3. Bring a large pot of water to a rolling boil. Salt abundantly and drop the pasta in gradually. Drain the lasagnette when al dente, transfer to a serving bowl or platter, and cover with the sauce. Toss well and sprinkle on the Parmigiano-Reggiano before serving.
   Serves 4

 # LASAGNE RICCE ALLE NOCI E FORMAGGI*

Ruffle-Edged Lasagne with Walnuts and Three Cheeses

This is a recipe without butter or olive oil. But the rich cheeses and walnuts make for an extremely satisfying preparation. Instead of making the free-form dish described below, you could also layer spoonfuls of the cheese-and-walnut mixture with the lasagne for a delicious concoction.

1 recipe Homemade White Flour and Egg Lasagne (page 10) or 1 pound commercial lasagne ricce
¼ pound gorgonzola cheese, at room temperature
¼ pound mascarpone cheese, at room temperature
⅔ cup freshly grated Parmigiano-Reggiano cheese
1 cup finely ground walnuts

1. Prepare the lasagne.

2. Bring a large pot of water to a rolling boil. Salt abundantly and drop the pasta in gradually.

3. Meanwhile, beat together the gorgonzola, mascarpone, Parmigiano-Reggiano, and walnuts in a mixing bowl.

4. Drain the lasagne when al dente and transfer to a serving bowl or platter. Toss with the cheese-and-nut mixture.

Serves 4 to 6

1. Prepare the lasagne.

2. Bring a large pot of water to a rolling boil. Salt abundantly and drop the pasta in gradually. Drain when the lasagne is al dente.

3. In a pan, place the butter and walnuts. Turn the heat to medium. Once the butter is completely melted, cook for 1 minute.

4. Transfer the lasagne to a serving bowl or platter and toss with the melted butter and walnuts. Sprinkle with the sugar, if desired.

Serves 4

 # LASAGNE RICCE ALLE NOCI*

Ruffle-Edged Lasagne with Walnuts

Housewives in the Friuli region of northeast Italy serve this lasagne as a first course. The delicious nutty butter flavor should not be unbalanced by too much sugar, so use only what is called for.

1 recipe Homemade White Flour and Egg Lasagne (page 10) or 1 pound commercial lasagne ricce
8 tablespoons unsalted butter
½ cup finely ground walnuts
½ teaspoon sugar (optional)

 # LASAGNE AL SUGO DI NOCI*

Lasagne with Nut Sauce

This very flavorful and textured free-form Sardinian lasagne recipe makes a nice first course.

1 recipe Homemade White Flour and Egg Lasagne (page 10) or 1 pound commercial lasagne
¼ cup olive oil
2 garlic cloves, peeled and finely chopped
¼ cup finely chopped fresh parsley
¼ cup fresh bread crumbs
2 cups ground walnuts
Salt

1. Prepare the lasagne.

2. Bring a large pot of water to a rolling boil. Salt abundantly and drop the pasta in gradually. Drain the lasagne when al dente.

3. Meanwhile, heat the olive oil in a casserole. Sauté the garlic, parsley, bread crumbs, walnuts, and salt to taste over medium-low heat for 10 to 12 minutes, stirring frequently.

4. Pour the lasagne into the casserole and toss well (but gently, if using fresh lasagne). Serve immediately.

Serves 4

 # LASAGNE AL SUGO DI FUNGHI*

Lasagne with Mushroom and Rosemary Sauce

This is a typical tossed lasagne preparation from Liguria. You can vary the recipe by adding prosciutto or finely chopped onions. If you happen upon the hard-to-find cèpes (*porcini*), by all means use them instead of the mushrooms called for.

1 recipe Homemade White Flour and Egg Lasagne (page 10) or 1 pound commercial lasagne
3 tablespoons unsalted butter

2 tablespoons olive oil
2 garlic cloves, peeled and finely chopped
2½ tablespoons finely chopped fresh parsley
2 tablespoons finely chopped fresh rosemary
1 pound ripe tomatoes, peeled, seeded, and chopped
¾ pound fresh cremini mushrooms, cleaned
2 tablespoons tomato paste
1 cup Beef Broth (page 28) or vegetable broth
¼ cup freshly grated Parmigiano-Reggiano cheese

1. Prepare the lasagne.

2. In a large casserole, place the butter and olive oil. Turn the heat to medium and when the butter is melted, sauté the garlic, parsley, and rosemary together for 1 minute, stirring constantly. Add the tomatoes and mushrooms, and mix well to coat. Dissolve the tomato paste in the broth and pour it into the casserole; stir well. Cover and cook 30 minutes, stirring occasionally. Turn the heat off and let the mushroom sauce sit for 10 minutes.

3. Meanwhile, bring a large pot of water to a rolling boil. Salt abundantly and drop the pasta in gradually. Drain when the lasagne is al dente, toss with the sauce, and cover with a sprinkling of Parmigiano-Reggiano. Serve immediately.

Serves 4 to 6

LASAGNE AL PESTO*
Lasagne with Pesto alla Genovese

The famous Genovese pesto is freshly made to season this lasagne alla genovese. Here I can recommend only freshly made lasagne and freshly made pesto, a combination so vastly superior to commercial lasagne and jarred pesto that it is analogous to the difference between a palazzo by Palladio and a Mussolini-era train station.

1 recipe Homemade White Flour and Egg Lasagne (page 10) or 1 pound commercial lasagne
1 recipe Pesto alla Genovese (page 27)

1. Prepare the lasagne.
2. Prepare the pesto.
3. Bring a large pot of water to a rolling boil. Salt abundantly and drop the pasta in gradually. Drain the lasagne when al dente but do not dry. Transfer to individual serving bowls or a large serving platter or bowl and spoon on the pesto.
Serves 4 to 6

 # LASAGNE AL BASILICO*
Lasagne with Basil, Walnuts, and Pecorino

This typical dish from Tuscany is another version of the previous recipe, Lasagne al Pesto. It too is a very easy tossed lasagne with a quick and strong pesto sauce, but its flavor is a bit different than that of Pesto alla Genovese (page 27).

1 recipe Homemade White Flour and Egg Lasagne (page 10) or 1 pound commercial lasagne
1 small bunch fresh basil (about 40 to 50 large leaves), washed and thoroughly dried
¾ cup shelled walnuts
1 cup freshly grated pecorino or pecorino Sardo cheese
6 tablespoons extra-virgin olive oil
Salt and freshly ground black pepper

1. Prepare the lasagne.
2. In a mortar, pound the basil, walnuts, and cheese until they form a thick paste. Slowly whisk in the olive oil, or use a food processor as in step 2 of Lasagne con Pesto alla Trapanese (page 89). Salt and pepper to taste.
3. Bring a large pot of water to a rolling boil. Salt abundantly and drop the pasta in gradually.

Drain the lasagne when al dente and transfer to a serving bowl or platter. Toss gently with the pesto and serve.

Serves 4

LASAGNE CON PESTO ALLA TRAPANESE*

Lasagne with

Trapani-Style Pesto

On the western coast of Sicily, in the city of Trapani, they make this almond and basil pesto for various shapes of pasta, including lasagne.

> *1 recipe Homemade Durum-Wheat and Water Lasagne (page 12) or 1 pound commercial lasagne*
> *4 ounces whole blanched almonds*
> *4 garlic cloves, peeled*
> *1 small bunch fresh basil (about 40 to 50 large leaves), washed and thoroughly dried*
> *Salt and freshly ground black pepper*
> *½ cup olive oil*
> *1 cup tomato puree*

1. Prepare the lasagne.
2. Grind together the almonds, garlic, basil, and salt and pepper to taste in a food processor.

While the machine is running, slowly add the olive oil in a thin stream. Process until the oil is completely incorporated and the mixture is well blended. Transfer to a mixing bowl and incorporate the tomato puree. You will have 1½ cups of pesto.

3. Bring a large pot of water to a rolling boil. Salt abundantly and drop the pasta in gradually. Drain the lasagne when al dente and transfer to a serving bowl or platter. Toss gently with the pesto and serve.

Serves 4

LASAGNE "A 'NTUPPU"*

Sicilian-Style Lasagne

with Tomato Sauce

A Sicilian recipe for homemade lasagne is dramatically enhanced by freshly grated ricotta salata, a hard, dried ricotta, instead of the more common Parmigiano-Reggiano or pecorino cheese. *'Ntuppu* is an old Sicilian word meaning stuffed with a stopper (the way a wine bottle is sealed with a cork), leading me to believe that originally this lasagne was closer to a kind of manicotti.

1 recipe Homemade Durum-Wheat and Water
    Lasagne (page 12) or 1 pound commercial
    lasagne
1 recipe Tomato Sauce (page 22)
1 cup grated ricotta salata

1. Prepare the lasagne.
2. Prepare the tomato sauce.
3. Bring a large pot of water to a rolling boil.
Salt abundantly and drop the pasta in gradually. Drain the lasagne when al dente and
transfer to a serving bowl or platter. Toss with
the tomato sauce and sprinkle with the ricotta
salata.
Serves 6

"MANDILLI DE SÊA"*

Ladies' Handkerchiefs

The name of this recipe is Ligurian dialect
for the shape of the lasagne—large 6-inch
squares, the size of a lady's handkerchief. This
dish can be seasoned with Pesto alla Genovese
or simply with butter and marjoram, as in
this preparation.

1 recipe Homemade White Flour and Egg
    Lasagne (page 10) or 1 pound commercial
    lasagne
8 tablespoons unsalted butter, melted

¼ cup finely chopped fresh marjoram
1 cup freshly grated Parmigiano-Reggiano cheese
1 recipe Pesto alla Genovese (page 27)
    (optional)

1. Prepare the lasagne. Cut into 4- or 6-inch
squares.
2. Mix the melted butter with the marjoram.
3. Bring a large pot of water to a rolling boil.
Salt abundantly and drop the pasta in gradually.
Drain the lasagne when al dente and transfer to
a serving bowl or platter, 1 sheet at a time, interspersing with butter and marjoram. Sprinkle
each layer with Parmigiano-Reggiano. Serve
immediately.
Serves 4

Note: If using pesto, toss gently with the lasagne.

LASAGNETTE AGLI SPINACI*

Lasagnette with Spinach

This pleasing dish looks as if it was made with
a pesto but is a simple preparation of spinach,
butter, and cheese. If you are unable to find
lasagnette, use lasagne.

1 recipe Homemade White Flour and Egg
    Lasagne (page 10) or ¾ pound commercial
    lasagnette

20 ounces spinach, stems removed and rinsed
  well
Salt
2 tablespoons olive oil
4 tablespoons unsalted butter
1 garlic clove, peeled and crushed
1 cup freshly grated Parmigiano-Reggiano cheese

1. Prepare the lasagne. Cut into ¾-inch-wide strips.

2. Rinse the spinach well and place in a pot without draining. Sprinkle with some salt. Turn the heat to high and cook until the spinach wilts, about 3 to 4 minutes. Drain well, pressing out excess water with the back of a spoon. Chop the spinach.

3. Heat the olive oil with the butter and garlic over medium heat in a medium sauté pan. When the garlic begins to turn light brown, remove and discard. Add the spinach with salt and pepper to taste. Cook the spinach for 4 minutes. Turn the heat off and sprinkle with half of the Parmigiano-Reggiano.

4. Meanwhile, bring a large pot of water to a rolling boil. Salt abundantly and drop the pasta in gradually. Drain when al dente and transfer to a serving bowl or platter. Toss the lasagnette with the spinach and serve with the remaining Parmigiano-Reggiano on the side.

Serves 4

 # "TACCÚNA CA SÁRSA 'NCUTUGNÁRI"*

Sicilian Twirled Lasagne with a Diavolo Sauce

From the Syracuse region of Sicily and the area around the baroque town of Noto comes a kind of lasagne called *taccúna*. The pasta is prepared in an unusual way: it is formed into a spiral that may once have been stuffed, from the old Sicilian word *'ncutugnári*. First the sheets of lasagne are liberally floured so they don't stick to one another; then they are cut into long strips, rolled around a thick stick, and left to dry for 2 hours. *Taccúna* perhaps comes from *taco*, the Spanish word for billiard cue, which may have once been used to twist the lasagne. This recipe calls for homemade lasagne made with durum wheat, salt, and water.

1 recipe Homemade Durum-Wheat and Water
  Lasagne (page 12) or 1 pound commercial
  lasagne
¼ cup olive oil
1 medium onion, peeled and finely chopped
2 pounds ripe plum tomatoes, peeled, seeded,
  and chopped
2 garlic cloves, peeled and crushed

*¼ teaspoon red chili pepper flakes or 1 to 2 fresh
red chili peppers, seeded and chopped*
3 tablespoons finely chopped fresh basil

1. Prepare the lasagne. Cut into 3 × 8-inch lengths. Dust each strip of lasagne liberally with flour and wrap around the handle of a wooden spoon or, if you desire authenticity, a billiard cue to dry.

2. In a casserole, heat the olive oil and sauté the onion over medium-high heat until golden, about 4 to 5 minutes, stirring frequently. Add the tomatoes, garlic, red chili pepper flakes or chili peppers, and basil, and cook for 10 to 12 minutes, adding up to ½ cup water if the sauce dries out too quickly.

3. Bring a large pot of water to a rolling boil. Salt abundantly and drop the pasta in gradually. Drain the lasagne when al dente and transfer to a deep serving bowl or platter. Cover with the sauce and serve.

Serves 4

 # "TACCÚNA CA MULINCIANA E RICOTTA"*

Sicilian Twirled Lasagne with Eggplant and Ricotta

Another tossed lasagne recipe typical of the baroque town of Noto, in southeastern Sicily, and featuring spiral lasagne. The tastes are rich and filling even though the preparation is very simple. It is best made with homemade lasagne. You need not follow the instructions in step 1 for shaping the lasagne; simply boil the lasagne in sheets. Ricotta salata is a hard, dried ricotta used for grating.

*1 recipe Homemade Durum-Wheat and Water
Lasagne (page 12) or 1 pound commercial
lasagne*
*1 medium eggplant (about 1¼ pounds), sliced
¼ inch thick*
1 recipe Tomato Sauce (page 22)
Pure olive oil or pomace for deep-frying
1 cup grated ricotta salata

1. Prepare the lasagne. Cut into 3 × 8-inch lengths. Dust each strip of lasagne liberally with flour and wrap around the handle of a wooden spoon or, if desired, a billiard cue.

2. Lay the eggplant slices on some paper towels and sprinkle with salt. Let them drain of their bitter juices for 1 hour or longer and then pat dry with paper towels.

3. Meanwhile, prepare the tomato sauce.

4. Heat the oil for frying to 375°F. Deep-fry the eggplant slices until golden brown, about 4 minutes a side. Remove, drain, and set aside.

5. Bring a large pot of water to a rolling boil. Salt abundantly and drop the pasta in gradually. Drain the lasagne when al dente and transfer to a deep serving bowl or platter. Cover with the fried eggplant, then the tomato sauce, and finally with the ricotta salata. Serve, tossing gently.

Serves 6

 # LASAGNE DI SAN GIUSEPPE*

San Giuseppe's Lasagne

Lasagne can become so specialized in terms of locale and occasion that there exist many kinds of lasagne in Italy to celebrate Saint Joseph's Day. One, from Cuneo, in the Piedmont, has layers of meat sauce and béchamel sauce and is baked with grated cheese and butter to form a golden crust.

Another, given below, is prepared in Bari, the capital of Apulia, at the opposite end of Italy, and is entirely different from that of Cuneo. This free-form lasagne is tossed with a sauce made of anchovies, tomatoes, basil, and garlic, and then sprinkled with fried fresh bread crumbs and finely ground almonds.

1 recipe Homemade Durum-Wheat and Water Lasagne (page 12) or 1 pound commercial lasagne
½ cup olive oil
1 garlic clove, peeled and crushed
10 large fresh basil leaves
1½ pounds ripe plum tomatoes, peeled, seeded, and chopped
Salt and freshly ground black pepper
1 cup fresh bread crumbs
12 salted anchovy fillets, rinsed
¼ cup whole blanched almonds, ground
Freshly ground black pepper

1. Prepare the lasagne.

2. In a large sauté pan, heat half of the olive oil over medium-high heat and sauté the garlic and basil together for 1 minute, stirring constantly. Add the tomatoes, salt and pepper to taste, and reduce the heat to low. Simmer for 45 minutes. Remove and discard the garlic.

3. In a small pan, heat 2 tablespoons of the olive oil and fry the bread crumbs over medium heat until golden, turning frequently. Remove the bread crumbs and set aside.

4. Bring a large pot of water to a rolling boil. Salt abundantly and drop the pasta in gradually. Drain the lasagne when al dente and transfer to a serving bowl or platter.

5. Meanwhile, pour the remaining olive oil into the same pan in which you cooked the bread crumbs and place over medium heat. Add the anchovies and once they have dissolved, return the reserved bread crumbs to the pan, together with the ground almonds, and stir for 2 minutes.

6. Pour the tomato sauce over the lasagne and then sprinkle on the bread-crumb mixture. Serve with freshly ground black pepper.

Serves 4

▧ LASAGNE ALLA SANREMESE*

Lasagne San Remo–Style

Porcini mushrooms are flavorful, and portobello mushrooms are large, dark, and meaty. In this preparation from Liguria, the mushrooms are simmered with some ripe tomatoes and then tossed with toasted bread crumbs, butter, and very thin sheets of lasagne. Then the lasagne is transferred to a warm serving bowl and interspersed with fresh basil leaves. The golden brown bread crumbs replace cheese in this dish.

1 recipe Homemade White Flour and Egg Lasagne (page 10) or ¾ pound commercial lasagne
¼ cup olive oil
8 tablespoons unsalted butter
1 small onion, peeled and chopped
2 garlic cloves, peeled and crushed
1 pound ripe plum tomatoes, peeled, seeded, and chopped
¾ pound fresh porcini or portobello mushrooms (or a mixture), cleaned and sliced
1 teaspoon dried oregano
Salt and freshly ground black pepper
⅓ cup fresh bread crumbs
20 large fresh basil leaves

1. Prepare the lasagne. Cut into 3-inch squares. Measure out ¾ pound and store the rest.

2. In a casserole, heat the olive oil with 2 tablespoons of the butter and sauté the onion and garlic over medium heat until the onion is soft, about 6 minutes, stirring frequently so the garlic doesn't burn. Add the tomatoes, reduce the heat to medium-low, and simmer 15 minutes.

3. Add the mushrooms, oregano, and salt and pepper to taste. Mix well. Cover, reduce the heat to low, and cook for 30 minutes, stirring occasionally.

4. Place the bread crumbs in a small pan and turn on the heat to medium-high. Brown the bread crumbs, shaking and stirring so they don't burn, about 5 minutes. Set aside.

5. Bring a large pot of water to a rolling boil. Salt abundantly and drop the pasta in gradually.

6. Butter a deep serving dish. Drain the lasagne when it is al dente and transfer to the casserole with the mushroom-tomato sauce.

Toss well but gently with the sauce, ¼ cup of the bread crumbs, the remaining butter, and some freshly ground black pepper to taste.

7. Ladle some lasagne into the buttered serving dish and sprinkle on a third of the basil. Add another few ladles and sprinkle on more basil. Ladle on the remaining ingredients and sprinkle the top with the remaining bread crumbs and several basil leaves. Serve immediately.

Serves 4

 # LASAGNETTE "ALL'AJADA"*
Lasagnette with Walnuts

Ajada is dialect in Lombardy for swaddling, indicating how the lasagne is to be cut: about 1½ inches wide, to resemble the bands of cloth with which the Madonna wrapped the infant Jesus. It is traditionally served in the lower Lombardy on Christmas Eve. The domain of this lasagne also extends into France, where in the Alpes-de-Haute Provence it is known as *crouzets* and eaten on Advent Eve.

This preparation is similar to one from the Veneto that uses fresh *bigoli,* a whole wheat spaghetti, instead of lasagne.

1 recipe White Flour and Egg Lasagne (page 10)
    or *1 pound commercial lasagnette*
3 garlic cloves, peeled

10 ounces shelled walnuts
1 cup fresh bread, torn into little pieces, white
    part only
½ cup milk
½ cup extra-virgin olive oil
½ teaspoon salt

1. Prepare the lasagne. Cut into 1½-inch-wide strips.

2. Place the garlic and walnuts in a food processor and grind coarsely. Transfer to a large mixing or serving bowl.

3. Soak the torn bread in the milk. Squeeze the milk out and mix the bread with the walnuts and garlic. Stir in the olive oil and salt.

4. Bring a large pot of water to a rolling boil. Salt abundantly and drop the pasta in gradually. Drain the lasagne when al dente and transfer to a serving bowl or platter, spooning some walnut mixture between each layer. Let the lasagne sit for a few minutes before serving.

Serves 4 to 6

LASAGNE AI SEMI DI PAPAVERO*

Poppy Seed Lasagne

This recipe is an Austrian legacy from the era when the Hapsburgs ruled the Friuli-Venezia Giulia region of the northeast. In Trieste, the region's capital, this preparation is also called by its German name, *Mohnnudeln* (poppy seed noodles), and the lasagne is left to rest for 24 hours before cooking. It is usually served as a first course.

> 1 recipe Homemade White Flour and Egg
>   Lasagne (page 10) or 1 pound commercial
>   lasagne
> 1 tablespoon poppy seeds
> 1½ tablespoons sugar
> 8 tablespoons unsalted butter
> Salt

1. Prepare the lasagne. Cut into 4-inch squares or 1½-inch-wide strips.

2. Bring a large pot of water to a rolling boil. Salt abundantly and drop the pasta in gradually. Drain the lasagne when al dente and transfer to a serving bowl or platter.

3. Meanwhile, pound the poppy seeds and sugar in a mortar until they form a powder, about 2 minutes of vigorous pounding. (A food processor is too big for this small amount, but a small electric coffee grinder works well.) In a small pan, melt the butter and cook the poppy seed mixture for 1 to 2 minutes over medium heat. Salt if you desire. Pour over the lasagne, toss quickly, and serve.

Serves 4

INDEX